LIGHTHOUSES
of the North East Coast

ROBIN JONES

HALSGROVE

First published in Great Britain in 2014

British Library Cataloguing-in-Publication Data
A CIP record for this title is available from the British Library

ISBN 978 0 85704 234 7

HALSGROVE

Halsgrove House,
Ryelands Business Park,
Bagley Road, Wellington, Somerset TA21 9PZ
Tel: 01823 653777   Fax: 01823 216796
email: sales@halsgrove.com

Part of the Halsgrove group of companies
Information on all Halsgrove titles is available at:
www.halsgrove.com

Printed in China by Everbest Printing Co Ltd

All in a day's work on
the coast of North
East England:
Seaham's harbour
lighthouse once again
defies rough seas.
KANE YOUNG

To Jenny, Ross and Vicky

CONTENTS

INTRODUCTION 5

1. BERWICK-ON-TWEED BREAKWATER 13
2. THE LINDISFARNE OBELISKS 17
3. BAMBURGH 21
4. THE FIRST FARNE LIGHTHOUSES 23
5. INNER FARNE AND BROWNSMAN 26
6. LONGSTONE AND GRACE DARLING 29
7. SEAHOUSES 36
8. WARKWORTH HARBOUR AND AMBLE 38
9. COQUET ISLAND 42
10. BLYTH 46
11. ST MARY'S ISLAND 51
12. TYNEMOUTH CASTLE 55
13. TYNEMOUTH AND SOUTH SHIELDS 58
14. NORTH SHIELDS 62
15. THE TYNE SWING BRIDGE 68
16. SOUTER 70

17. SUNDERLAND 74
18. SEAHAM 82
19. HARTLEPOOL AND SEATON CAREW 84
20. SEAL SANDS 91
21. SOUTH GARE AND REDCAR 93
22. WHITBY HARBOUR 97
23. WHITBY HIGH 103
24. SCARBOROUGH 106
25. FLAMBOROUGH HEAD 111
26. BRIDLINGTON 115
27. WITHERNSEA 117
28. SPURN HEAD 122
29. SPURN AND OTHER HUMBER LIGHT VESSELS 129
30. THORNGUMBALD CLOUGH 136
31. PAULL 139
32. SALT END 141
33. WHITGIFT 142

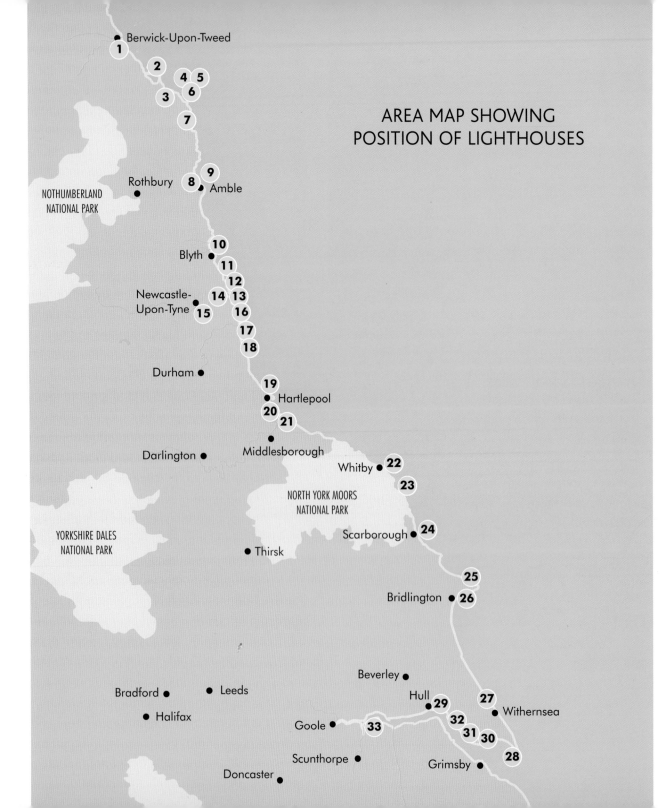

AREA MAP SHOWING POSITION OF LIGHTHOUSES

Berwick-Upon-Tweed
1
2
4 5
3 6
7

NOTHUMBERLAND NATIONAL PARK

Rothbury
8 9
Amble

Blyth
10
11
12
Newcastle-
Upon-Tyne
14 13
15 16
17
18

Durham

19
Hartlepool
20
21

Darlington
Middlesborough

Whitby 22
23

NORTH YORK MOORS NATIONAL PARK

YORKSHIRE DALES NATIONAL PARK

Scarborough 24

Thirsk

25

Bridlington 26

Beverley

Bradford   Leeds

Hull
29
27
Withernsea

Halifax

Goole
33
32
31 30
28

Scunthorpe

Doncaster

Grimsby

INTRODUCTION

BRITAIN HAS MANY excellent reasons to be proud of the North East of England, for it was a region that changed the face of the globe through its transport technology.

The roots of so much of the modern age can be found in Durham, Tyneside, Northumberland and Yorkshire. Not only did the wholesale extraction of minerals from the coalfields there fuel the great furnaces of the Industrial Revolution, but also provided the impetus for developing a new form of fast cheap transhipment of materials, in the form of the steam railway.

The region is known as the cradle of the railways. It was there that George Stephenson, his son Robert and their contemporaries took the invention of Cornish mining engineer Richard Trevithick and developed it into a machine which could replace horses as traction on the scores of mineral tramways that served the mines, colliers and ports in the region.

In 1825, the world's first public steam-operated line, the Stockton & Darlington Railway was opened. Steam railways enabled vast bulk loads of raw materials to be shipped quickly and efficiently to the ports and harbours of the North East, and once Britain's national network took shape, trains returned with imports from both abroad and elsewhere along the coast, along with the fruits of the then-vast fishing fleets. Later still, railways brought visitors en masse to coastal towns where resorts sprang up.

However, it was not all plain sailing – far from it. The coast of the North East has been described as one of the most dangerous in the British Isles, because of the high number of shipwrecks.

The North Sea had for centuries provided a vital line of communication between Scotland and Edinburgh and England and London, not only for trade but for the conveyance of passengers. In the days before the coming of the railways, when stagecoaches were state-of-the-art, journeys between the two capital cities would take days. Before the creation of turnpike roads, many of the routes were muddy potholed affairs, and travellers were at risk of being waylaid by highwaymen.

As for the carriage of minerals in bulk, forget it. When a canal network linked the growing industrial cities of the Midlands and Yorkshire with London and ports like Liverpool and Bristol the

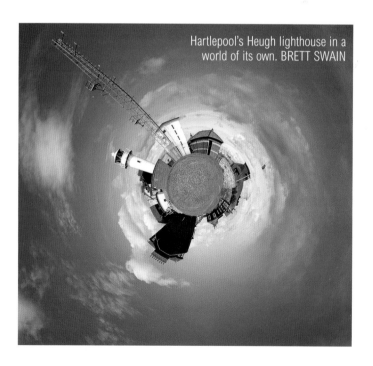

Hartlepool's Heugh lighthouse in a world of its own. BRETT SWAIN

Lighthouses like this one at South Gare near Redcar were designed to take the worst that nature can throw at them.
DAVID PYE

North East found itself left out. The only way to trade in sizeable commodities was by sea.

For centuries, shipwrecks had been by-and-large taken as par for the course, a hard fact of life as far as traders were concerned. However, with the upsurge in cargoes being carried from the ports of the North East, there was a corresponding rise in the number of wrecks, leading to increasingly vitriolic demands from business-men, ship owners, mariners and their families for action to be taken, in the form of better navigational aids. At one stage it was said that there were an average of 44 wrecks per mile on this coast.

The earliest recorded lighthouse in England is the surviving Roman pharos at Dover. However, since the Romans departed our shores, the building of lighthouses ceased until around 1328, when St Catherine's Oratory on St Catherine's Down near the southern coast of the Isle of Wight was built by the Lord of Chale, Walter de Godeton, as penance for plundering wine from a shipwreck.

Throughout Britain, there are numerous historical examples of local landowners or entrepreneurs applying to build lighthouses in a bid to improve safety at sea by providing marks which could warn sailors off rocks, shoals and sandbanks twenty-four hours a day.

So many colliers sailors between Newcastle and London were lost in the 17th century, including in a devastating storm of 1695, as recorded by *Robinson Crusoe* author Daniel Defoe, that collier owners demanded several lighthouses be built on the route, beginning with one at Lowestoft in 1609.

From a modern-day viewpoint, anyone wishing to build a lighthouse would surely be welcomed with open arms, but the opposite was so often the case. The owner of a lighthouse would normally expect to be paid dues by passing ships for providing a safe navigation aid, and the maritime authorities, mainly Trinity House in London and also the separate organisations of the same name in Newcastle-upon-Tyne and Hull, remained vehemently opposed to such profiteering. In some instances, it was a case of not wanting anyone else to benefit from money which they felt should be rightly theirs. In others, the opposition was out of genuine concerns about how useful the promised lights were.

Medieval lights were most often braziers in which coal or

wood was burned to create a beacon, or candle-lit affairs? There were fears about how effective they would be, if the light did not burn brightly enough, was extinguished in the wind, or not properly maintained.

Trinity House came into being in 1514 when Henry VIII granted it a royal charter under the name "The Master, Wardens, and Assistants of the Guild, Fraternity, or Brotherhood of the most glorious and undivided Trinity, and of St Clement in the Parish of Deptford-Strond in the County of Kent." It was granted as a result of a petition placed on 19 March, 1513 by a guild of Deptford-based mariners who asked the king for a licence to regulate pilotage because of the poor conduct of unregulated pilots on the Thames.

Today, Trinity House performs a triple role. It is the General Lighthouse Authority for England, Wales, the Channel Islands and Gibraltar, responsible for a range of general aids to navigation ranging from lighthouses to radar beacons.

It is also a charity dedicated to the safety, welfare and training of mariners. Lastly, it is also a deep sea pilotage authority, licensing expert navigators to act as deep sea pilots for ships trading in northern European waters. Trinity House also inspects buoys provided by local harbour authorities.

On 4 January, 1505, a group of seafarers formed a charitable guild, originally named the "Guild of the Blessed Trinity of Newcastle upon Tyne, on the quayside of Newcastle to support the town's growing maritime community and their dependents.

At the time, the River Tyne was described as "a tortuous, shallow stream, full of sand shoals, impeding flow from the harbour entrance up to Walker, with the river as high as Newcastle fordable at low tide". The Brethren of Newcastle's Trinity House used their expertise to bear in improving standards and facilities on the waterway.

The Newcastle Trinity House, which is based in the city's Broad Chare, received the first of seven royal charters on 5 October, 1536, also from Henry VIII. This first charter allowed the Brethren to impose dues on ships trading into the Tyne at the rate of two pence per English ship and four pence per foreign

The coat of arms of London's Trinity House. ROBIN JONES

Trinity House keeper Terry Johns in the garden of Coquet Island lighthouse. COURTESY DR PAUL G MORRISON

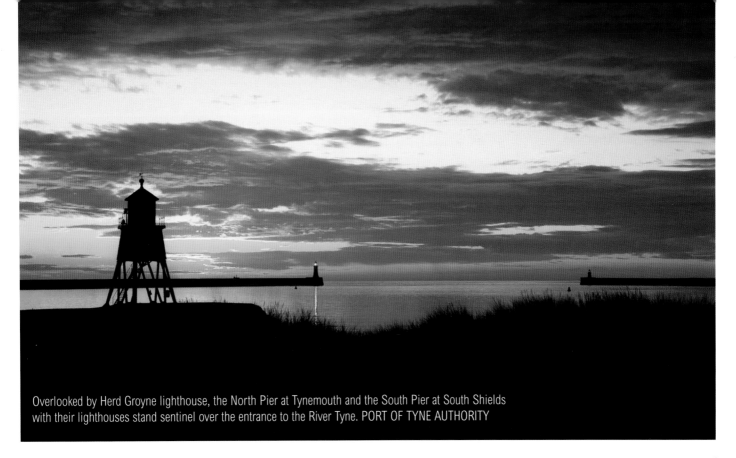

Overlooked by Herd Groyne lighthouse, the North Pier at Tynemouth and the South Pier at South Shields with their lighthouses stand sentinel over the entrance to the River Tyne. PORT OF TYNE AUTHORITY

ship. In exchange, the Brethren had to "build, fortify, moat, embattle and garrison two towers on the north side of the entrance to the river Tyne." These towers were to have navigational lights and were the original High and Low Lights at North Shields, as described in Chapter 14.

Newcastle's Trinity House eventually took responsibility from Berwick-upon-Tweed in the north to Whitby in the south. It established buoys and beacons, licensed shipmasters, mates and pilots, advised and carried out improvements to rivers and ports.

Beginning in 1883 the house gradually lost control of its lights and buoys to local river and harbour authorities. The last such transference of power was that of buoys and seamarks around Holy Island to London's Trinity House in 1995.

The Trinity House is now an active examining and licensing authority for deep sea pilots, qualified to operate from Gibraltar to the North Cape, as well as assisting with the examination of local pilots and supplying maritime expertise elsewhere.

Hull also has a Trinity House, dating back to 1169, when 27 parishioners from Holy Trinity Church agreed to offer mutual assistance when required. In 1369, this group was formalised as a guild of 49 men and women. It has administered alms houses since 1457 and today provides 64 rest homes for needy seamen or their widows, and pays out 700 pensions.

In 1512, Hull shipmasters requested the Brethren to supply "good men" to pilot "strange" ships into and out of Hull. Under a royal charter issued by Henry VIII in 1541, all foreign ships were to be piloted into Hull by the Brethren.

Under a charter of Elizabeth I, in 1581 the organisation became known as "The Guild or Fraternity (Brotherhood) of Masters and pilots, Seamen of the Trinity House in Kingston-upon-Hull". A second charter from the queen gave the Hull Trinity House authority to settle seamen's wages disputes, and examine and licence masters and pilots, and in 1584, the Lord High Admiral issued a proclamation empowering it to establish buoys and beacons, and to collect dues for their maintenance. Its first buoy was set in the Humber along with two beacons in 1613, and in 1832, the Bull lightship became the first on the estuary.

To mark the 600th anniversary in 1969 of the foundation of the Guild, the Queen, Prince Philip, Prince Charles and Princess Anne visited Hull Trinity House.

The modern era of lighthouse building is widely held to have begun at the start of the 18th century, in many cases driven by necessity as coastal, European and transatlantic commerce boomed in the wake of the Industrial Revolution, with bigger ships carrying payloads that mariners would at one time have barely dreamed possible.

Advances in structural engineering and new and efficient lighting equipment paved the way for bigger and more powerful lighthouses to be built, including ones that could stand everything the sea could throw at it: take a look at the pictures of those at Sunderland, Seaham or South Gare to see how crucial this factor was on the coastline covered in this book.

A revolutionary step in lighthouse design came in 1782 when Swiss scientist Aimé Argand produced his Argand lamp which emitted a steady smokeless flame, burning whale oil, colza, olive or other vegetable oil. First produced by Matthew Boulton, in

The entrance to Hull's Trinity House. It has occupied the present site in Trinity House Lane, a short walk from Hull Marina, since 1467, and was enlarged in 1737, during the reign of George II, as indicated over the door of the main entrance. ROBIN JONES

A two-wick Argand lamp displayed in the National Maritime Museum at Greenwich. These lamps paved the way for modern lighthouse design. ROBIN JONES

A vaporised oil burner, of a type improved by David Hood, displayed in the National Maritime Museum at Greenwich. First invented in 1901, this lamp mixed paraffin and air through an incandescent mantle made from a woven fabric. Combined with a lens, it could produce a length with an intensity of a million candle power or candela. It was in use in British lighthouses until 1975. ROBIN JONES

VAPORIZED OIL BURNER
improved design by David Hood,
in use between 1922 and 1975

The long-disused lighthouse in the Humberside village of Paull. ROBIN JONES

partnership with Argand, in 1784 and became a standard fitting for lighthouses for more than a century.

The Argand lamp paved the way for optical lenses to increase and focus the light intensity, concentrating the light into a beam and vastly increasing its visibility. The first such apparatus, known as a catoptric system, was developed by William Hutchinson in 1763. In turn it led to the first revolving lighthouse beams, whereby the light would appear to ships in a series of intermittent flashes. It also became possible to transmit complex signals using the light flashes.

French physicist and engineer Augustin-Jean Fresnel developed the multi-part Fresnel lens for use in lighthouses. His design permitted the construction of compact lenses with a bigger apertures and shorter focal length, while capturing more oblique light from a light source, the net result being that a lighthouse using his system could be seen from a greater distance.

The age of coal braziers was over.

The vaporised oil burner was invented in 1901 by Arthur Kitson, and improved by David Hood at Trinity House. It produced more than six times the luminosity of traditional oil lights.

Gas lighting for lighthouses became widely available with the invention of the Dalén light by Swedish engineer, Gustaf Dalén. He also invented the 'sun valve', which automatically regulated the light and turned it off during the daytime. This apparatus became the predominant form of light source in lighthouses from the 1900s through to the 1960s, by which time it had been overtaken by electricity.

Electrification and automatic lamp changers made lighthouse and lightship keepers redundant. The last manned lighthouse in the British Isles was at North Foreland in Kent, automated in 1998. Today, Trinity House controls its aids to navigation from its Operations and Planning Centre in Harwich by telemetry.

Improvements in maritime navigation and Global Positioning Systems have all helped to make lighthouses redundant. There remains those who have their doubts, wondering what happens when the GPS system breaks down.

The public at large love lighthouses. They are popular with photographers, painters and even poets, and the whole of Britain and way beyond was inspired by keeper's daughter Grace Darling who defied tempestuous seas to rescue survivors from an 1838 shipwreck in the Farne Islands, as detailed in Chapter 6. Lighthouses are a focal point of the skyline in many towns, and despite being declared obsolete, they are by no means useless, being converted into museums and visitor centres and even holiday accommodation.

Britain is a great seafaring nation, and lighthouses are an essential part of its proud national tradition and heritage.

The sun sets beyond the start of the Humber, watched over by Spurn Head lighthouse. NIGEL WALKER*

CHAPTER 1
BERWICK-ON-TWEED BREAKWATER

OUR JOURNEY BEGINS in the great frontier town of Berwick-on-Tweed, a town that has changed hands between England and Scotland many times in history. It was last conquered by England in 1482, since when it has had the unique position of being the former county town of Berwickshire, which lies in another country, the border of which is 2½ miles to the north.

The Angles created the Dark Ages kingdom of Bernicia, which amalgamated with Deira to form Northumbria. The part of the kingdom north of the River Tweed, the 97-mile long great salmon river which tries its best to form a natural border, was given to the Scots who defeated the Northumbrians at the Battle of Carham in 1018.

A frontier town has, of course, to have a great castle, and so did Berwick, on the north bank of the Tweed. It was there on 17 November 1292 that the claim of spider-loving Robert the Bruce to the Scottish crown was declined by Edward I of England, who had won the first Battle of Dunbar that year, in favour of John Baliol.

Between 1174 and 1482, when it was captured by the future Richard III, Berwick 'bounced' between England and Scotland more than 13 times, and Edward I returned in 1296, brutally sacking the town. The town was a prize jewel, for by that time it had become one of the wealthiest trading ports in Scotland, exporting wool, grain and salmon. Scottish coins were minted there.

The reign of Elizabeth I saw vast sums of money spent on fortifying Berwick, with a new rampart wall around the town.

Berwick was the first English town to greet James VI of Scotland on his way to being crowned James I of England in 1603. When he crossed Berwick Bridge, legend has it he stated that the town was neither English nor Scottish but belonged to the united Crown. Its place in England was finally settled by the Act of Union of the two countries in 1707.

Berwick remained a county in its own right, and was not included in Northumberland for Parliamentary purposes until 1885.

In recent years, there have been rumblings from Members of the Scottish Parliament for Berwick to be returned yet again, and

A 19th-century view of Berwick breakwater's lighthouse, from *The Ports, Harbours, Watering-Places and Picturesque Scenery of Great Britain* by William Finden.

The pier at Berwick harbour on a stormy November day, prior to the repainting of the lighthouse in 2013.
KAREN V BRYAN*

surveys suggested a majority of the population might be in favour.

However, as of 2014, Berwick is not only the northernmost town in England, with the most northerly railway station – 335 miles north of King's Cross and 55 miles south of Edinburgh – but also the country's northernmost lighthouse.

During the 19th century, Berwick again became an important trading town. Its main industries include tourism, salmon fishing, shipbuilding, engineering, sawmilling and – what else – tweed manufacture!

It grew in size with the addition of new harbours and quays. Starting in 1810, and taking eleven years, the 960ft breakwater on the north side of the river was built on the foundations of the remains of a previous one said to have been built in the reign of Elizabeth I, to protect the entrance to the Tweed from the sea. Stone was extracted from local quarries near Spittal and was shipped across from the south side of the Tweed to the pier workings. The pier was built by the great Scottish engineer John Rennie.

Berwick Harbour Commissioners, first agreed to investigate the possibility of building a lighthouse at its end, to guide boats in and out of the Tweed, at their meeting on September 19, 1825.

At first, John Smeaton, who had built the third Eddystone lighthouse, was invited to build it, but did not take up the offer. Instead, it was designed by Joseph Nelson, (1777-1833), who had also been responsible for two lighthouses on Inner Farne in the Farne Islands during 1809-10 and the one at Longstone Rock in 1826.

A native of Birstall near Batley in Yorkshire, where he came from a family of stonemasons, Nelson was associated with at least 15 lighthouses. We first hear of him as the builder of Anglesey's South Stack lighthouse, designed by Daniel Asher Alexander in 1809, surveyor to Trinity House. Nelson was also responsible for building the wooden low light at Burnham-on-Sea, which features on the cover of sister volume *Lighthouses of the South West*, also published by Halsgrove.

The foundation stone was laid on 17 February, 1826 by Admiral Stow and the 43ft round stone tower, capped with a conical roof comprising a single piece of stone, was completed

Good as new: the lighthouse as repainted by Iain Grieve.
KAREN V BRYAN*

later that year.

The reflector from the original oil lamp is displayed in Berwick Museum, but the glass chimney has been broken.

At first, two lights, one above the other, were exhibited at night. The upper one, of a pale, white colour, was lit from sunset to sunrise, while the lower bright red one was a tide light, and displayed only when there was ten feet water on the bar.

Eventually, oil was replaced by gas. Then came electricity, but the huge batteries which powered the light had to be charged up at a garage in the town. The charge lasted only a week, and so every Friday, a set of recharged batteries was brought out by wheelbarrow to the tower. Today, however, it is powered by a mains supply.

On the landward end of the pier stands the keeper's cottage, occupied for several generations by the Wilson family.

As well as the pier and lighthouse, other harbour works were completed, but the hoped-for rise in the port's prosperity failed to materialise. A combination of increased harbour dues to pay for the works and the decline in the salmon catch – caused by the size of the harbour mouth being reduced by the construction of the new pier, which discouraged salmon from entering – have been cited as reasons. However, the pier which affords views across to the Farne Islands became popular with holidaymakers and birdwatchers, and postcards depicting its lighthouse sold well for decades.

The tower is painted white, with the base and lantern in red. At the front is a wide window, from which the main white light is displayed, with a focal plane (the height of a light above mean high water) of 49ft.

In front of the window is the gallery, which until 2011 housed a fog detector and foghorn.

Today, the seaward light flashes once every five seconds, and is visible for 10 nautical miles, while a small fixed green light is shown from a window in the back of the tower, facing inland and visible for 1 nautical mile.

In 2011, local painter and decorator Iain Grieve gathered a consortium of businessmen together to repaint the lighthouse, which looked shabby due to prolonged exposure to the elements. The commissioners did not have the budget for the repaint so Iain, a fundraiser for Berwick Rotary Club and the Round Table and his colleagues stepped in.

"The lighthouse is such an iconic building and as a company we've weathered the recession reasonably well so I wanted to put something back into the community," he said.

A rainbow appears behind Berwick breakwater and its lighthouse, while the wind whips up a flurry of sand on Spittal beach in front of the waves. GAVIN BURTON*

CHAPTER 2
THE LINDISFARNE OBELISKS

A CRADLE OF Celtic Christianity, a shining beacon of wisdom and learning that breaks the gloom of the Dark Ages, Lindisfarne is the island jewel of the north of England.

Linked by a tidal causeway covered twice a day, and situated within the Northumbrian Coast Area of Outstanding Natural Beauty the name may have been derived from 'farne', meaning 'retreat' – the island became used as such by holy men for centuries – and Lindis, a nearby river.

Inhabited since the Stone Age, the first recorded settler was an Irish monk named St Aidan who arrived there in 635 and founded a monastery.

Oswald, the Christian second son of the pagan Northumbrian King Aethelfrith, ascended to the throne in 633 and made nearby Bamburgh his stronghold. He invited the monks of the island of Iona off the west coast of Scotland, where St Columba had founded a monastery, to move to Lindisfarne, where Aidan set up a community with 12 brethren. From Lindisfarne, Aidan's monks went out converting the heathen population of England.

West Old Law and East Old Law obelisks were built to guide mariners safely into Holy Island harbour. GLEN BOWMAN*

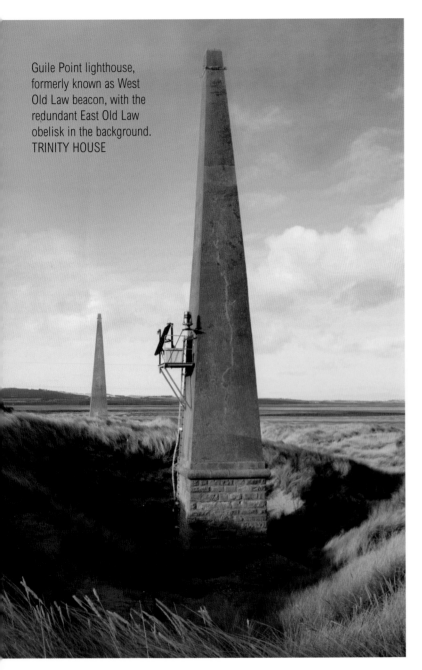

Guile Point lighthouse, formerly known as West Old Law beacon, with the redundant East Old Law obelisk in the background.
TRINITY HOUSE

Aidan died at Bamburgh in 651, to be succeeded by St Cuthbert, whose miracles and life were recorded by the Venerable Bede.

Cuthbert acquired medieval cult status, and it is believed that the Lindisfarne Gospels, one of the world's greatest treasures of literature from this period, were written in the late seventh century in honour of him, possibly by Eadfrith, an island monk who became bishop of Lindisfarne in 698.

Lindisfarne's darkest hour came on 8 January, 793 when the island was pillaged by the Vikings and the monks killed or sold into slavery, Monks would, however, one day return to Lindisfarne. The priory was re-established in Norman times as a Benedictine house and survived until its suppression by Henry VIII in 1536.

At the highest point of the island stands the 16th century Lindisfarne Castle, built using some of the stones from the priory, as part of an English defence against the Scots.

Lindisfarne today may be renowned for its classic coastal splendour, but the lime kilns are testament to times when it was a hive of industry. Limestone was quarried and the stone brought to the kilns via a waggonway and burned to make lime, a popular agricultural fertiliser.

At its height in the mid-19th century, more than 100 men were engaged in quarrying on the island. Coal was also carried from the island's harbour, which in the early 19th century began to become congested.

In response to the appalling loss of life along this stretch of coast, when 700 sailors' lives were lost in one year, Trinity House of Newcastle-upon-Tyne, which had responsibility for the building and maintenance of local lighthouses, beacons and buoys, finally took steps to tackle the problem at Holy Island.

In the first decade of the 19th century, Newcastle's Trinity House ordered the building of a white brick 35ft pyramid on a 10ft cliff which forms part of Emmanuel Head at the north eastern extremity of the Holy Island. Historians have conjectured that this structure, which was never used as a conventional lighthouse, was Britain's first daymark.

The harbour at Holy Island, a treacherous destination until daymarks were erected.
FRIENDS OF ORTHODOXY

The stone daymark on Emmanuel Head.
RICK CROWLEY*

The beach-bound East Old Law beacon.
TRINITY HOUSE

The modern Heugh Hill lighthouse which
replaced East Old Law beacon. TRINITY HOUSE

One of the principal causes of shipwrecks was a nearby headland which resembled Emmanuel Head: it became known as the "False Emmanuel Head." This daymark was intended to distinguish the real one from the lookalike.

Around the same time, Trinity House of Newcastle also decided to erect a pair of unlit beacons at Old Law on the sand dunes at Guile Point to act as beacons; when seaman lined them up, the safe channel on the southern approach to the harbour was indicated.

The first pair of beacons were wooden towers, and between 1820-40, possibly around 1829, they were replaced by a pair of brick obelisks designed by John Dobson and sited around 120ft to the east.

The building of the obelisks which stand 122 yards apart proved to be a colossal task, not just with the shipping in of raw materials from North Shields, but ferrying workmen from the island to the tidal site in all weathers

The obelisks are known as East Old Law (70ft high) and West Old Law (83ft) and at first each was topped by a wrought iron triangle on a metal staff.

West Old Law was repaired in 1937 after being struck by lightning.

On 1 November, 1995, the pair passed from the control of the local Trinity House to the main one in London.

Since they were built, the channels leading to the harbour have shifted and the alignment of the pair is no longer meaningful.

Since 1992, the West Old Law obelisk shines a fixed light about a third of the way up and is known as Guile Point lighthouse. It has a focal plane of around 29ft.

East Old Law is effectively redundant: its job in marking the channel into the harbour is now undertaken by a modern light positioned on a steel lattice structure and which is named Heugh Hill lighthouse.

Synchronised with Guile Point lighthouse, Heugh Hill flashes a white, red and green light every six seconds. It has a range of 4 nautical miles.

Spectacular Bamburgh Castle dates from Norman times. In the late 18th century, a set of bells and guns to warn mariners was set up on its ramparts.
GAIL JOHNSON/VISITNORTHUMBERLAND.COM

CHAPTER 3
BAMBURGH

IMPOSING GRADE I-listed Bamburgh Castle was built by the Normans on a basalt outcrop which had been strategically occupied since prehistoric times. A British fortress in the fifth century, it was captured by the Anglo-Saxon ruler Ida of Bernicia in 547. Ida's grandson Aethelfrith gave it to his wife Bebba: her name was taken by the nearby settlement Bebbanburgh, which became Bamburgh.

Lying only 20 miles from the English border, the castle has also been fought over by the Danes and the kings of Mercia and Northumbria.

After William II unsuccessfully laid siege to the later castle in 1095 during a rebellion backed by its owner, Robert de Mowbray, Earl of Northumbria, his wife surrendered it after he was captured. It then passed to the English crown.

It was crucial in England's defence against raids from Scotland, and during the Wars of the Roses, it became the first castle in England to be defeated by artillery, after being besieged for nine months by Richard Neville, 16th Earl of Warwick.

Thomas Malory, writer of Arthurian legends, considered Bamburgh to be Sir Lancelot's castle Joyous Gard. The castle fell into decay but was restored by various owners during the 18th and 19th centuries. In the late 18th century it became a charity school run by a Doctor Sharp, who also set up various measures to improve the safety of passing ships.

He set up an elementary lifeboat station in Bamburgh Village, in addition to installing a warning system of bells and guns on the castle ramparts.

During fierce gales, he had two riders patrolling the shore to keep watch for ships in distress.

The restoration of the castle was completed by Victorian industrialist William Armstrong in 1900, the year of his death. His family still live there today.

Visitors who take the public tour can see the museum room, king's hall, cross hall, armoury and the Victorian scullery. Since the 1920s it has also been used as a film location for several period dramas.

Above: The original Bamburgh lighthouse of 1910.
AUTHOR'S COLLECTION

Below left: Bamburgh's modern-day unmanned lighthouse of Black Rock Point, with Inner Farne on the horizon. DAVID EMSLEY/TRINITY HOUSE

Below right: The small lighthouse sits just below Bamburgh golf course. The light on top is enclosed in a black cylinder. TRINITY HOUSE

In 1910, a 42ft lighthouse was built on the shore front at Black Rock Point in Bamburgh as part of a late Victorian scheme to complete the chain of coastal lighthouses. Its immediate purpose was to guide ships passing along the Northumberland coast and in the turbulent waters around the Farne Islands

This first lighthouse was a circular skeletal metal-framed affair illuminated by acetylene gas lamps from a stone-built carbide store next door.

It was converted to electricity in the mid-sixties and turned off in 1975. In its place, a light was placed on top of the disused white-painted carbide store, and the old lighthouse was removed.

It is the most northerly land-based lighthouse in England. Unmanned, a local attendant undertakes routine maintenance of the light which is monitored from the Trinity House Operations & Planning Centre at Harwich in Essex.

The 30ft high light has a focal plane of 41ft and an intensity of 7,140 candela. Its occulting white, red and green light flashes twice every eight seconds from a cluster of three 50 watt tungsten halogen lamps through a 1st order catadioptric fixed lens. It can be seen for 12 miles.

CHAPTER 4
THE FIRST FARNE LIGHTHOUSES

THE FARNE ISLANDS, a scattered Northumbrian archipelago of rocky islets, became internationally famous in early Victorian times because of the heroics of Grace Darling, a lighthouse keeper's daughter.

In 1838 she became a national celebrity after helping her father rescue nine survivors from a stricken steamer by rowing a small boat through tumultuous seas from their home on remote Longstone lighthouse, risking their own lives in the process.

However, much more of Grace soon.

The little archipelago of islands takes its name from Farne, the largest of 28 islets and rocky outcrops and the one which is nearest to the mainland.

They are scattered between 1½ and 4¾ of a mile from the coast. Small the cluster of islands may be, but they lie directly in main deep water coastal shipping lanes, and for centuries have presented a serious danger to navigation. Those that lie unseen at high tide present the greatest threat.

The islands are divided into the Inner Group and the Outer Group, which are divided by Staple Sound.

The main islands in the Inner Group are Inner Farne, Knoxes Reef and the East and West Wideopens, and at very low tides they are joined together, while the Outer Group includes Staple Island, the Brownsman, North and South Wamses, Big Harcar and the Longstone. The highest point, on Inner Farne, is 62ft above sea level.

The Farnes are the most easterly outcrop of the Great Whin Sill, a strip of hard volcanic rock that stretches through Northumberland. They became islands when sea levels rose after the last Ice Age: composed of unyielding igneous dolomite, they were left intact when weaker limestone was eroded by the sea,

Prior Castell's Tower was an early lighthouse on Inner Farne.
MIKE MARSTON

leaving them detached from the mainland. The steep columns formed by fissured dolomite gives the islands their steep and often vertical cliffs, with stacks up to 66ft high.

Some of the islands are capable of supporting vegetation because of a clay subsoil and peat soil, but others are just barren rock.

Despite their isolation, particularly in times of severe weather, the islands have attracted human habitation, most

An early 20th-century view of Prior Castell's Tower and St Cuthbert's chapel. AUTHOR'S COLLECTION

famously in the form of early Christian monks, many connected with Lindisfarne, and who followed the old Celtic tradition of island hermitages.

The islands were first recorded in 651, when they became home to St Aidan, followed by St Cuthbert, who became Bishop of Lindisfarne but returned after two years to spend the final years of his life in solitude on Inner Farne, where he died in 687. Cuthbert had introduced special laws in 676 protecting eider ducks and other seabirds nesting on the Farne Islands, and they are thought to be the world's earliest bird protection laws. Eider ducks are also known as cuddy ducks because of their link with the saint. Remains still exist of the cell used by Aiden and Cuthbert.

The final monastic cell on the islands was established by Benedictine monks in 1255 and lasted until Henry VIII dissolved the monasteries in 1536, after which the islands became the property of the dean and chapter of Durham Cathedral. In 1894, they were bought by industrialist William Armstrong, the same who lived at Bamburgh Castle. Today, the islands are owned by the National Trust.

It was in 1673 that in a bid to improve navigational safety around the islands, Sir John Clayton built a tower on Inner Farne as part of a planned chain of lighthouses for the east coast, after obtaining a patent for it four years earlier.

King Charles II, granted a licence to erect a beacon, and it is said that Prior Castell's Tower, an existing peel or pele tower, had a coal fire built on top.

Peel towers are small fortified keeps or tower houses, built in the border country and north of England to act as watch towers. By an Act of Parliament of 1455, these towers were required to have an iron basket on their summits and a smoke or fire signal, for day or night use, to be lit by a garrison to warn of approaching danger.

These towers were also used by local landowners as homes, and in times of peril, the surrounding village could take refuge inside.

Around 1540, Thomas Castell, prior of Durham, (1494-1519), built the large square peel tower on Inner Farne to house monks, next to St Cuthbert's chapel. After the monasteries were dissolved, it became a fort, and according to some reports, around 1673 the tower became a lighthouse, a century before Blackett.

Clayton's scheme failed because the merchants of Newcastle-upon-Tyne refused to pay tolls for its maintenance, despite efforts by the Elder Brethren of Trinity House to reach an agreement, and so the fire in the brazier was never lit.

Clayton also planned lighthouses for Flamborough Head, Foulness near Cromer and two at Corton near Lowestfoft. Only the latter pair ever shone a light, and lasted from 1675-78.

Proposals for a lighthouse on the Farne Islands were drawn up again in 1727, this time by coastal traders, but again they came to nothing. A scheme mooted by the islands' leaseholder Captain John Blackett in 1755 also failed for the same reason as Clayton's.

However, in 1776 Blackett reached agreement with Trinity House to build two lighthouses at his own expense, one on Inner Farne and the other at the southern end of Staple Island.

At Inner Farne, he used the four-storey peel tower, again with a coal fire built on top.

On Staple Island, a small cottage with a light on the roof was built by Blackett as his other navigational aid.

Lights were said to have been first shone from the pair on 1 December, 1778, with coal fires providing the illumination.

Gales blew down the Staples Island light in 1784. A replacement was built, in 1791, on adjacent Brownsman's Island. Reports suggest it had to be rebuilt after being washed away by raging seas in 1800.

This 39ft rubblestone tower emitted light from a coal-burning grate on top.

Robert Darling, the keeper of the Staple Island cottage lighthouse, moved with his family to Brownsman Island.

By 1809, it was obvious that both of these lighthouses were falling into disrepair and were inadequate for purpose.

Trinity House took them over and made plans for new lights.

Prior Castell's Tower stands behind St Cuthbert's chapel on Inner Farne.
FRIENDS OF ORTHODOXY

CHAPTER 5
INNER FARNE AND BROWNSMAN

TRINITY HOUSE replaced the ailing two lighthouses on Inner Farne Island and Brownsman Island by building three.

Daniel Asher Alexander, who had succeeded Samuel Wyatt as consultant engineer to Trinity House in 1807, designed the existing lighthouse on Inner Farne which was built in 1811.

His first lighthouse had been South Stack on Anglesey in 1809, and also in 1811 he built one on the German island of Heligoland, which has been in British hands since 1807 when it surrendered during the Napoleonic Wars.

Alexander was also the architect of Dartmoor and Maidstone prisons, two of Britain's oldest jails still in use today.

Inner Farne lighthouse, a low, compact station perched above a sheer cliff face, with a circular brick tower nearly 43ft high and painted white, was the larger of a pair on the island which worked in conjunction. At 2 ½ miles out to sea, it is the nearest to the mainland of all the Farne Islands lights. The second one built by Alexander on Inner Farne was a smaller 27ft octagonal wooden tower 500ft away on the north-west point of the island.

Adjoining the main lighthouse is a large white flat-roofed rectangular building for generating acetylene, and single-storey keepers' houses. The whole station is surrounded by a stone wall.

At first, Argand lamps and reflectors produced a fixed white light.

Between 1810-11, Alexander built a new oil-powered

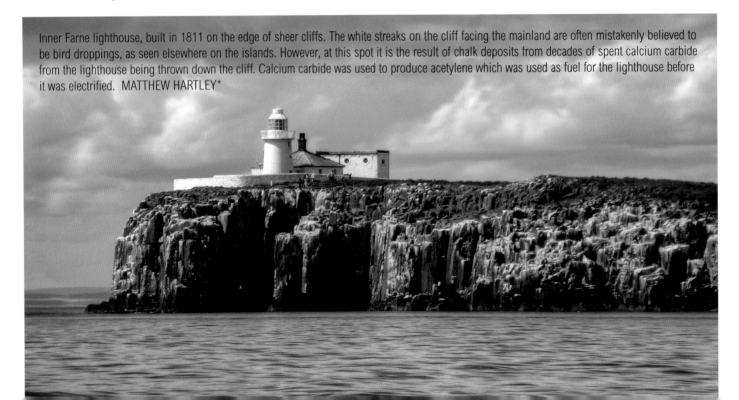

Inner Farne lighthouse, built in 1811 on the edge of sheer cliffs. The white streaks on the cliff facing the mainland are often mistakenly believed to be bird droppings, as seen elsewhere on the islands. However, at this spot it is the result of chalk deposits from decades of spent calcium carbide from the lighthouse being thrown down the cliff. Calcium carbide was used to produce acetylene which was used as fuel for the lighthouse before it was electrified. MATTHEW HARTLEY*

Inner Farne lighthouse today,
with the array of solar panels
which power it to the left.
TRINITY HOUSE

lighthouse on Brownsman Island, replacing the previous tower, until it was superseded by a new lighthouse on Longstone Rock in 1826. The new Brownsman tower on the other side of the keeper's cottage replaced the earlier one, which became a storehouse.

The smaller Inner Farne light was discontinued and demolished in 1910, when the unmanned lighthouse at Bamburgh became operational. A short white-painted brick circular tower lighthouse with a traditional light and buildings attached is currently operated by Trinity House.

In 1825 Trinity House bought out the lease of the lights on Inner Farne from the Blackett family for £36,484.

Inner Farne's main lighthouse in 1910 became one of the first run by Trinity House to be automated. It was equipped with a 'sun valve' which cut off the acetylene gas supply in the day and turned it back on at night. This simple procedure remained in use until 2006, when solar panels were installed during modernisation.

Nowadays, the lighthouse is equipped with a 1st order catadioptric fixed lens which from a 50 watt tungsten halogen lamp shows a white light of 1,650 candela with a range of 10 nautical miles, and a red sector of 208 candela between 136 and 292 degrees visible for 7 nautical miles. There are two white and red flashes every fifteen seconds.

The National Trust bought the lighthouse from Trinity House for £132,000 in 2005, and converted some of the buildings into offices, although the light remains operational. It is controlled and monitored via a telemetry link from the Trinity House Operations and Planning Centre at Harwich.

The remains of the lighthouse on Brownsman's Island which was built in 1811 and used until 1826. The base of the tower can be seen to the right of the keeper's cottage. The large square tower is the earlier lighthouse which after 1811 became a storehouse. The cottage is now used by the National Trust.
TIM PARKINSON*

CHAPTER 6
LONGSTONE AND GRACE DARLING

IN 1826, TRINITY HOUSE ordered the building of a lighthouse on the almost barren and very bleak Longstone Rock.

Designed and built by Joseph Nelson, who also built the Berwick-on-Tweed breakwater light amongst several others, Longstone lighthouse comprises a red and white-painted rough stone circular tower, with iron railings around its lantern gallery.

The first survey for a light on the rock was undertaken in March 1825, and under the direction of Nelson and his foreman Thomas Wade, who both lived with the Darling family on Brownsman Island while the work was underway, the tower was completed that December. The pair and their workmen had raced against time to complete it before the first ravages of the winter set in.

On 29 September that year, Hugh Percy, 3rd Duke of Northumberland, and Vice-Admiral of the Coast, arrived in his cutter-rigged yacht to view the lighthouse. Largely renowned elsewhere for his haughtiness towards common people, the duke showed great interest in the building work and was friendly to those involved. He struck up a friendship with William Darling, the lighthouse keeper, and several letters which subsequently passed between them have been preserved. The duke expressed interest in the lives of the Darling family which comprised Grace, her eight brothers and sisters and mother and father, and showed respect and admiration for their spartan existence in isolation.

Joseph Nelson's Longstone lighthouse today.
MIKE ROBINSON/
TRINITY HOUSE

The 83ft tall lighthouse and the keeper's dwellings cost Trinity House £4,771 to build. The lantern itself cost £1,441.

The first light was shone from Longstone in 1826. It was provided by Argand lamps with 12 burners, parabolic reflectors 21in in diameter and 9in deep and a catadioptric optical apparatus.

After it was completed, the Darling family moved from Brownsman Island to take over the new lighthouse, although they regularly returned to collect food and vegetables from the garden at their old home.

Alexander's Brownsman tower was subsequently demolished to avoid confusion with the new one at Longstone, although the ground floor room survives as an adjunct to the keeper's cottage.

The Farne Islands are renowned as the home of the eider duck, Britain's biggest and fastest flying duck, and a protected species. Grace tended them: her mother Thomasin used their feathers to fill mattresses, and it is likely that the family ate them too, despite St Cuthbert's protective edict as mentioned earlier.

Indeed, the islands are world famous for their wildlife, and between April and early August burst into life with the cries of sea birds, with around 100,000 nesting pairs. Puffins use the same burrows as rabbits but at different times of the year: long ago introduced as a source of meat, a common practice on smaller islands, the rabbits have since gone wild.

Arctic, common and sandwich tern and the rare roseate tern, razorbill and guillemot, oystercatcher, shag, kittiwake, fulmar greater and lesser black-backed gull, rock pipit, ringed plover, cormorant and gannet contribute to a total of 290 bird species recorded on the islands. Other rare sightings included, in 1760, the now-extinct great auk, and in 1979, an Aleutian tern from the north Pacific, the only example of the species ever recorded in Europe.

An Arctic tern chick ringed by conservationists on the islands in 1982 turned up in Melbourne, Australia three months later, having completed one of the world's longest recorded journeys by a bird.

Grace learned how to row the family's small coble, a type of craft that needs at least three people to row properly in rough seas, repair fishing nets and carry out other physical seafaring work.

While her elder brothers and sisters left to live on the mainland at Bamburgh or elsewhere, Grace, her younger brother William Brooks Darling and parents stayed on Longstone where they maintained their simple lifestyle, which very few people if any today would find palatable.

During storms the waves occasionally covered the living rooms on the lower floors, and they sought refuge in the upper rooms of the tower.

Looking out of an upstairs window of Longstone lighthouse early on 7 September, 1838, because she could not sleep during a particularly vicious storm, Grace spotted the wreck of the SS *Forfarshire*.

The steamer was bound from Hull to Dundee when it went aground on Hawkers Rocks, about a mile from the lighthouse.

The stern of the vessel was split off and carried away in the storm during the night, and 43 people were drowned. Nine survivors clung to the remaining part which was lodged on the rocks.

William Darling also saw the wreck at daybreak, as did fishermen on the mainland, but all of them thought that it was impossible to attempt a rescue because of the sheer force of the waves smashing against the rocks.

However, believing that the lifeboat at Seahouses would not launch in such rough weather, Grace persuaded her father to at least try, and offered to be the second hand in the lighthouse's 21ft coble.

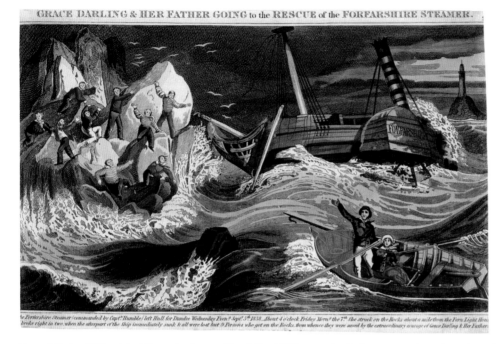

GRACE DARLING & HER FATHER GOING to the RESCUE of the FORFARSHIRE STEAMER.

Above left: An 1838 print of Grace Darling and her father William rowing to the rescue of survivors from the SS *Forfarshire*.
NATIONAL MARITIME MUSEUM, LONDON

Above right: Grace Darling's bravery made her one of Britain's all-time greatest heroines, inspiring countless books, articles and souvenirs.

Opposite: A statuette of Grace Darling. NATIONAL MARITIME MUSEUM, LONDON

In their flimsy vessel, the pair eventually reached the islet of Big Harcar, where they took on board four men and a woman whose two children had died on the ship.

William rowed back to the lighthouse with three of the men while Grace and the fourth man comforted the woman, a Mrs Dawson. William then rowed with two of the ship's crew back to the wreck to collect the remaining survivors.

The Seahouses lifeboat set out after all, only to arrive at the wreck after the Darlings. By then it was too dangerous to return, so the lifeboat's crew of seven fishermen, which included Grace's brother William Brooks, who had been ashore on the night of the storm, took shelter at the lighthouse. They remained at Longstone lighthouse for nearly three days before it was possible to safely return to the mainland.

Nine other passengers and crew members had earlier escaped the stricken steamer by lifeboat and were picked up by a passing ship.

The Times summed up the thoughts of an admiring nation on 19 September, 1838, when it commented: "Is there in the whole field of history, or in fiction even, one instance of female heroism to compare with this?"

The whole nation was inspired for generations to come by the heroics of Grace, who was awarded an RNLI silver medal for bravery.

Gold medals were awarded to both Grace and her father by the Royal Humane Society along with £50 from Queen Victoria.

Her exploits that night inspired William Wordsworth to write his poem *Grace Darling* in 1843.

> AMONG the dwellers in the silent fields
> The natural heart is touched, and public way
> And crowded street resound with ballad strains,
> Inspired by ONE whose very name bespeaks
> Favour divine, exalting human love;
> Whom, since her birth on bleak Northumbria's coast,
> Known unto few but prized as far as known,
> A single Act endears to high and low
> Through the whole land—to Manhood, moved in spite
> Of the world's freezing cares—to generous Youth— 10
> To Infancy, that lisps her praise—to Age
> Whose eye reflects it, glistening through a tear
> Of tremulous admiration. Such true fame
> Awaits her 'now'; but, verily, good deeds
> Do not imperishable record find
> Save in the rolls of heaven, where hers may live
> A theme for angels, when they celebrate
> The high-souled virtues which forgetful earth
> Has witnessed. Oh! that winds and waves could speak
> Of things which their united power called forth 20
> From the pure depths of her humanity!
> A Maiden gentle, yet, at duty's call,
> Firm and unflinching, as the Lighthouse reared
> On the Island-rock, her lonely dwelling-place;
> Or like the invincible Rock itself that braves,
> Age after age, the hostile elements,
> As when it guarded holy Cuthbert's cell.
>
> All night the storm had raged, nor ceased, nor paused,
> When, as day broke, the Maid, through misty air,
> Espies far off a Wreck, amid the surf, 30
> Beating on one of those disastrous isles—
> Half of a Vessel, half—no more; the rest
> Had vanished, swallowed up with all that there
> Had for the common safety striven in vain,
> Or thither thronged for refuge. With quick glance
> Daughter and Sire through optic-glass discern,
> Clinging about the remnant of this Ship,
> Creatures—how precious in the Maiden's sight!
> For whom, belike, the old Man grieves still more
> Than for their fellow-sufferers engulfed 40
> Where every parting agony is hushed,
> And hope and fear mix not in further strife.
> "But courage, Father! let us out to sea—
> A few may yet be saved." The Daughter's words,
> Her earnest tone, and look beaming with faith,
> Dispel the Father's doubts: nor do they lack
> The noble-minded Mother's helping hand
> To launch the boat; and with her blessing cheered,
> And inwardly sustained by silent prayer,
> Together they put forth, Father and Child! 50
> Each grasps an oar, and struggling on they go—
> Rivals in effort; and, alike intent
> Here to elude and there surmount, they watch
> The billows lengthening, mutually crossed
> And shattered, and re-gathering their might;
> As if the tumult, by the Almighty's will
> Were, in the conscious sea, roused and prolonged
> That woman's fortitude—so tried, so proved—
> May brighten more and more!
>   True to the mark,
> They stem the current of that perilous gorge,
> Their arms still strengthening with the strengthening
>   heart, 60

The lenses inside Longstone lighthouse. JAMES WEST*

Longstone Rock lighthouse – still giving sterling service the best part of two centuries after Grace Darling's heroic rescue. TRINITY HOUSE

Boat trips to Longstone lighthouse are run from the mainland. The lighthouse is now maintained by Trinity House via its local attendant who provides guided tours inside it. Visitors can view Grace's tiny bedroom from where she spotted the survivors. PETER MULLIGAN*

Though danger, as the Wreck is neared, becomes
More imminent. Not unseen do they approach;
And rapture, with varieties of fear
Incessantly conflicting, thrills the frames
Of those who, in that dauntless energy,
Foretaste deliverance; but the least perturbed
Can scarcely trust his eyes, when he perceives
That of the pair—tossed on the waves to bring
Hope to the hopeless, to the dying, life—
One is a Woman, a poor earthly sister,   70
Or, be the Visitant other than she seems,
A guardian Spirit sent from pitying Heaven,
In woman's shape. But why prolong the tale,
Casting weak words amid a host of thoughts
Armed to repel them? Every hazard faced
And difficulty mastered, with resolve
That no one breathing should be left to perish,
This last remainder of the crew are all
Placed in the little boat, then o'er the deep
Are safely borne, landed upon the beach,   80
And, in fulfilment of God's mercy, lodged
Within the sheltering Lighthouse.—Shout, ye Waves
Send forth a song of triumph. Waves and Winds,
Exult in this deliverance wrought through faith
In Him whose Providence your rage hath served!
Ye screaming Sea-mews, in the concert join!
And would that some immortal Voice—a Voice
Fitly attuned to all that gratitude
Breathes out from floor or couch, through pallid lips
Of the survivors—to the clouds might bear—   90
Blended with praise of that parental love,
Beneath whose watchful eye the Maiden grew
Pious and pure, modest and yet so brave,
Though young so wise, though meek so resolute—
Might carry to the clouds and to the stars,
Yea, to celestial Choirs, GRACE DARLING'S name!

Many other books, articles, paintings and souvenirs enhanced the legend that built up around her.

Grace died from tuberculosis in 1842, aged just twenty-six. She is buried with her father and mother in a grave at St Aidan's church in Bamburgh, where a cenotaph was erected in her memory.

The Royal National Lifeboat Institution has a Grace Darling Museum at Bamburgh, while the Seahouses lifeboat is named after her.

William Brooks Darling became keeper at Longstone lighthouse after his father retired.

In 1952, the lighthouse was converted to electricity after major alterations were made.

Above left: Grace Darling's grave in Bamburgh churchyard.
NICHOLAS JACKSON*
Above right: The memorial to Grace Darling at Bamburgh.
NICHOLAS JACKSON*

The interior of the Grace Darling Museum at Bamburgh, showing a Northumberland coble rowing boat, of the type that would have been used by Grace Darling and her father. RNLI

It was converted to automatic operation in September 1990 and is now also monitored from Harwich.

The light has a focal plane of 75ft and a range of 24 nautical miles. Through its small 3rd order catadioptric twin spectacle lens, one white flash is emitted every twenty seconds.

In May 2014, Northumberland County Council granted planning permission to Trinity House to install 27 solar panels on the nearby accommodation block.

The original plan involved a vertical-axis wind turbine and solar panels being mounted on the walls of the Grade II-listed lighthouse, but council planners advised against it. The revised plan had the solar panels installed at 10 degrees to the horizontal so that they do not protrude above the parapet wall.

Once the panels are in place, the diesel generators which currently run full time will be used only to supplement the solar power.

The entrance to the Royal National Lifeboat Institution's Grace Darling Museum. RNLI

CHAPTER 7
SEAHOUSES

A PRIMARY GATEWAY to the Farne Islands and a tourist draw in its own right is the sizeable village and small port of Seahouses.

Situated within the Northumberland Coast Area of Outstanding Natural Beauty, and also known as North Sunderland, it is from here that many pleasure trips to the islands are run, and it is where Trinity House's local lighthouse attendant has a quayside store for supplies and equipment.

Seahouses is a centre for ornithology, scuba diving, sea angling and some commercial fishing. It also has an annual Seahouses Festival, which started out in 1999 as a celebration of sea shanties. Between 1898 and 1951, Seahouses was the north-eastern terminus of the North Sunderland Railway.

Its small harbour is protected by breakwater piers. At the far end of the north-west pier stands an unmanned 30ft hexagonal white-painted brick tower lighthouse with a slightly curved domed roof and a window for a light.

The sole purpose of the light, which was built in 1900, is to guide boats in and out of the harbour.

Operated by North Sunderland Harbour Commissioners, the light has a focal plane of 36ft and shows a continuous green light visible for 12 miles.

Right, main: The harbour at Seahouses beneath an ominous sky.
JULIE PEARSON

Inset left: The unmanned lighthouse on the Seahouses breakwater pier.
STEVE FAREHAM*

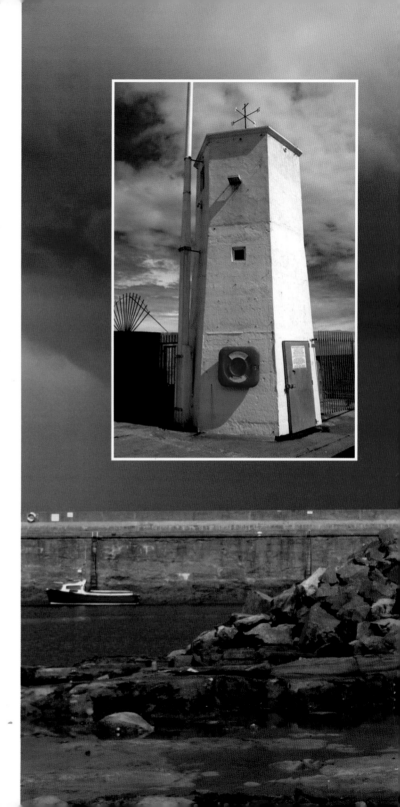

Dawn breaks over Seahouses harbour, with its breakwater lighthouse. FARNE.CO.UK*

CHAPTER 8
WARKWORTH HARBOUR AND AMBLE

BETWEEN 1838-49, a harbour was built by engineer John Rennie at the mouth of the River Coquet, which in 1765 had changed its course after a storm and from then on entered the sea at Amble.

A fishing port grew up around what had been a small hamlet until 1837 when the Warkworth Harbour Commission was set up to make improvements. Warkworth is the name of the town further up the river, and the newly upgraded port took on the name of Warkworth harbour.

Two breakwaters either side of the river mouth were built, the longest, the northern one, originally being 2,300ft in length. The piers were built using local stone but it proved unsuitable and was replaced with Scotttish granite when they were rebuilt.

After a branch line to Amble was opened by the York, Newcastle & Berwick Railway in September 1849, coal staithes were built. The harbour became the smallest and northernmost of those serving the coalfields of Northumberland and Durham.

By 1914, around 500,000 tons of coal were exported from Amble, an extremely modest figure when compared to the ports to the south.

Industries such as shipbuilding and fishing grew as little Amble expanded, and the town also had a brickworks. The coal traffic has now gone, the railway having closed in the '60s, but the fishing industry continues, albeit in a reduced form, and Amble has long since taken off as a small seaside resort.

Amble South Pier lighthouse at sunset.
PAUL MORRISON

Amble or South Pier lighthouse bears the brunt of a rough sea.
JACOB BAX

The piers and lights at Warkworth harbour in 1915, when it was a
coal port. AUTHOR'S COLLECTION

Amble Marina was opened in 1987 and a new fish dock was constructed in 1988 to cater for the fleet of cobles and seine netters of the port's fishing fleet.

Lifeboats have been based at Amble since 1842, because of the dangers presented by this stretch of coastline. Between 30 and 40 people died in shipwrecks near the port on 17–18 December, 1872.

The ambiguous name for the harbour has resulted in the northern pier being known as Warkworth breakwater and the south one as Amble breakwater. Each has a lighthouse at its end.

The pair operates in tandem with Coquet Island which lies offshore, and which is described in the next chapter. The island lighthouse guides ships towards the correct approach to the harbour, and the pier lights indicate the deepwater channel.

Lighthouse stations were established on both pierheads in 1848. The North Pier has a 26ft square skeletal tower with a gallery and enclosed upper section.

With a focal plane of 39ft, it emits a green flash every six seconds. The light is run off solar power and can be seen for 5 miles.

The South Pier has a 28ft round cast-iron post light with a gallery, mounted on a circular concrete base and painted with red and white horizontal bands. A concrete catwalk leads to the structure.

With a 30ft focal plane, it emits a red flash every five seconds which is also visible for five miles.

The harbour is still operated by the Warkworth Harbour Commissioners. Funded by English Partnerships, the South Pier was completely refurbished and the work was completed early in 2000. It was officially reopened by football legend Jack Charlton on May 21 that year.

A flock of seagulls swoops around North Pier or Warkworth lighthouse. JACOB BAX

CHAPTER 9
COQUET ISLAND

COQUET ISLAND lies a mile offshore, the nearest town being Amble. The 15-acre isle, a low tract of green pastureland, was, like Lindisfarne and the Farne islands, sought as a place of solitude by holy men as long ago as the seventh century.

Abbess Elflaeda of Whitby visited St Cuthbert there in 684, persuading him to accept the bishopric of Lindisfarne. In Norman times, the island was home to St Henry of Coquet, a Danish nobleman who wished to found a hermitage and was allowed to live on Coquet by the monks of Tynemouth.

He became famous as a prophet, and many travelled to Coquet to seek his advice. He died in 1127 and was enshrined at Tynemouth.

While Henry gave out a beacon of hope to the world around him, the building where he lived now emits a beacon of light to seafarers, for much of his Benedictine monastery was incorporated into the island's lighthouse, built in 1841 on the south western shore by Trinity House at a cost of £3,268 (along with the attendant keepers' cottages).

Self sufficiency: lighthouse staff pictured with their allotments in 1902. COURTESY DR PAUL G. MORRISON

Sunset over Coquet Island and its lighthouse.
DR PAUL G. MORRISON

The lighthouse with its distinctive 72ft white square sandstone tower was built to the design of James Walker. The tower is surrounded by a turreted parapet with walls more than a yard thick, the whole complex giving the appearance of a fortress.

Among the remains of the monastery is the unpainted stone base of the lighthouse, which is therefore part of a Scheduled Ancient Monument.

The island is owned by the Duke of Northumberland and was bought by his family in 1753. The castellated appearance of the lighthouse is not unlike a castle, and the battlements of Syon House, the duke's London residence, are made of sandstone from the island.

Other Grade II listed buildings include a Napoleonic gun battery with an explosives store which was used to keep the charges for the fog signal, and the crenallated garden walls.

The first keeper appointed to the lighthouse was William Darling, elder brother of Grace Darling, and the second of her brothers to become a Trinity House keeper.

Until the 1920s, the keepers and their families lived on the island and kept pigs, hens and goats, growing their own vegetables using seaweed as a natural fertiliser.

There were two wells to supply fresh water while rainwater was also collected from the roof of the lighthouse. Fresh water came from two wells and they also collected rain water from the roof of the castellated lighthouse.

In 1999, the lighthouse became automatic with no resident keeper, and is now operated by Trinity House from its base at Harwich in Essex.

The light has been solar powered since 2008. With a focal plane of 82ft, the lighthouse currently has a 1st order catadioptric fixed lens emitting a white light with an intensity of 155,000 candela and a range of 21 miles, and a red light with an intensity of 21,830 candela visible for 17 miles. The characteristic is the white and red lights flashing three times every twenty seconds. The fog signal sounds a three-second blast every thirty seconds.

The island is now uninhabited in winter and managed by the Royal Society for the Protection of Birds. Its wardens are present on Coquet throughout the summer to protect the nesting birds, using the keepers' cottages.

As a highly environmentally-sensitive nature reserve which contains important colonies of common and arctic terns, fulmars, black-legged kittiwakes, three kinds of seagull and eider ducks, the general public are barred from landing on the island.

However, Amble-based trip boats run as close to the island as possible, so visitors can see and photograph the lighthouse and birds from the sea.

The most numerous species is the puffin, with more than 18,000 pairs nesting. Most important is the colony of the at-risk roseate tern, which thanks to conservation attempts expanded to around 100 pairs during the first decade of the 21st century. Coquet now has 90 per cent of Britain's roseate tern population.

The old radio room houses the telemetry equipment which relays information on the state of the lighthouse electronics to Trinity House control room at Harwich. DR PAUL G. MORRISON

Coquet Island is paradise for seagulls,
and many other species of seabirds too!
DR PAUL G. MORRISON

CHAPTER 10
BLYTH

BLYTH HAS BEEN a port since the 12th century, but it was only about 300 years ago that the modern town we know today, with a population of around 36,000, began to take shape.

In 1723, Matthew White a prominent merchant of Newcastle-upon-Tyne and his brother-in-law, Richard Ridley of Blagdon bought huge swathes of land in the Blyth area under the banner of their company they had founded, Richard Ridley & Co., which was heavily involved with the coal trade, salt manufacture and shipping.

By 1730, two quays, one for coal and the other for ballast, a pilots' watch house and a lighthouse, of which no details survive, had been built by Richard Ridley at Blyth harbour. The first breakwater was built in 1765, and in 1788 the first coal staith with an elevated loading point was erected.

White's son Sir Matthew White, who was made a baronet in 1756, never married and died in 1763. His sister Elizabeth married their first cousin Matthew Ridley, son of Richard, who was MP for Newcastle five times over, Governor of the Newcastle-upon-Tyne Company of Merchant Adventurers and four times mayor,

Their son Sir Matthew White Ridley, 2nd Baronet (1745-1813), who became immortalised in a verse of the popular song The Keel Row as the "bright star of Heaton", became MP for Morpeth in 1768, and mayor of Newcastle six years later, when he won the parliamentary seat of that town which had been previously held by his father. Amongst his close friends was the American general and presidential candidate Charles Cotesworth Pinckney, who sent him a copy of the US constitution before it was passed.

Sir Matthew White Ridley, who owned Cowpen Colliery, furthered the development of the port of Blyth. It was also in

1788 that he designed Blyth High Light.

When first built, the High Light stood on the quayside and was 35ft tall. The white-painted slightly-tapered circular brick tower had a window for a light as opposed to a lantern gallery, and illumination was provided by oil lamps.

The light could be seen for 10 nautical miles. It is ascended by means of an internal spiral staircase.

The development of the Cowpen Quay and Waterloo areas began in about 1810 and 1815 respectively, and during Victorian times, major house building took place there.

Much development took place around South Harbour, which was completed in 1882. The light from Ridley's tower became obscured by new buildings.

As a result, it was heightened by 14ft in 1888, and again by 12.5ft in 1900, bringing it up to its present height of 61.5ft.

Land reclamation saw the shore 'move' outwards by around 100ft from the site of the High Light, which now stands as an annexe to a house in Bath Terrace just above the quay.

Dawn breaks behind Blyth's East Pier, as the lighthouse emits its beam. In 1992, Blyth Harbour Wind Farm was constructed alongside the pier. Consisting of nine wind turbines and with a maximum capacity of 2.7 megawatts, it provided enough electricity for over 1,500 homes. In 2012, the first of a new generation of turbines was installed as part of a scheme to replace the original nine with seven. It alone generates up to 3.4 megawatts, more power than all nine of the old turbines combined. CHARLOTTE ASTRID*

The High Light became the leading light for a series of other harbour lights, most of which have since disappeared. There was a Low Light, which was rebuilt in 1936, a 26ft hexagonal stone tower with a circular window just below its roof.

In the 1890s, the tidal inlet known as "the Slake" or "the Flanker" which divided old Blyth from Cowpen was filled in. Before then, the two areas were linked only by Waterloo Bridge, but once the creek was no more, the two areas merged into each other and the town took its present shape.

Coal had been exported from Blyth for centuries, and by 1855, a quarter of a million tons of coal were being shipped from the town, rising to three million by 1900. By 1914, Blyth was the major port for the export of Northumbrian coal. Tonnage rose to 5.5 million by 1930 and six million by the early 1960s. Fishing, shipping and the salt trade (until it died out in 1876) also contributed to the port's growth.

In 1847, the port was linked to collieries at Seghill by a railway, and Blyth's first station opened. Seghill was already linked to North Tyneside by rail, and the two lines merged to become the Blyth & Tyne Railway, which had a resounding impact on the prosperity of the port.

The Blyth Harbour and Docks Board was formed in 1853, and five years later, the Harbour Act was passed allowing dredging of the harbour to begin.

The Blyth Harbour Commission was formed in 1882, after new coal loading staiths and the South Harbour were built.

In the first half of the 20th century, Blyth was one of the largest shipbuilding yards on the North East coast, and built many ships for the Royal Navy during both world wars, including the first aircraft carrier, HMS *Ark Royal* in 1914. It also became a submarine base during both conflicts.

The port went into decline in the 1960s, with the rail link being closed under the Beeching Axe. The last local colliery, Bates Pit, closed in 1986, and in January 2002, Blyth Power Station, which dated from 1958, was declared redundant.

Blyth High Light was built in 1788 and was discontinued in 1985. The tower stands in Bath Terrace, just above the quay.
CHRISTINE WESTERBACK*

Blyth in the late 19th century, as sketched in Finden's *Views Of The Ports, Harbours and Watering Places Of Great Britain*. The volume describes the "lighthouse of stone", and the "basket light" to its left of it, in which lights are exhibited at night when there is 8ft of water on the bar.

Although the major industries which 'made' Blyth have largely vanished, the harbour thrives, shipping paper and pulp from Scandinavia for the UK newspaper industry, while handling container traffic and the import of materials used for aluminium production.

The port today is operated by Port of Blyth, the operating division of Blyth Harbour Commission. As a trust port, it is governed by its own local legislation under the control of an independent board.

Blyth High Light had been upgraded to gas in 1857, and in 1932 was supplied with electricity. It gave sterling service until July 1984, when it along with the Low Light was discontinued, the pair having been superseded by modern navigation aids on a different alignment. The Low Light was demolished around that time, and replaced with lattice posts. The High Light was then repainted mushroom instead of white and afforded Grade II listed building protection on 15 July 1987. It is now one of the oldest structures in the port.

The Daleks have landed in Blyth! This old crumbling wooden white painted shed located on the north side of the Blyth estuary opposite Low Quay is the Blyth Snook Range front light. JACOB BAX

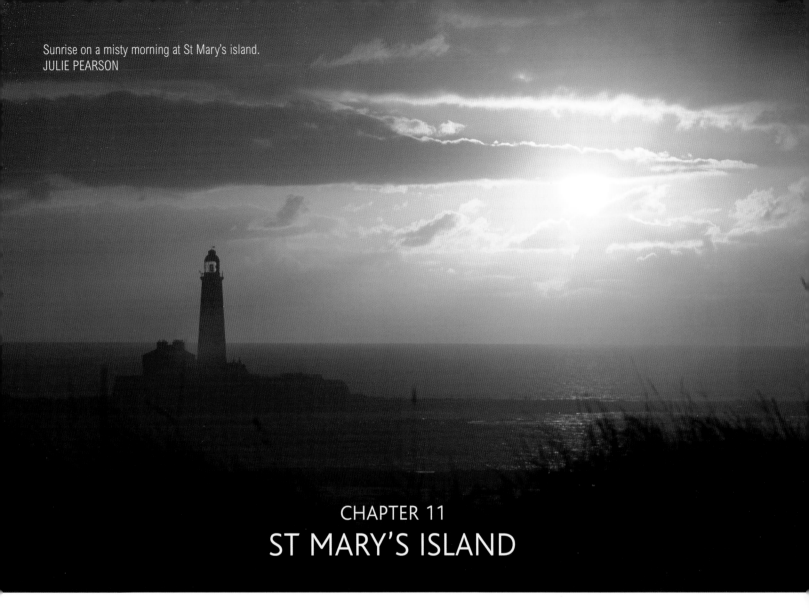

Sunrise on a misty morning at St Mary's island.
JULIE PEARSON

CHAPTER 11
ST MARY'S ISLAND

TINY ST MARY'S Island which lies on the coast between Whitley Bay and Seaton Sluice is a hugely popular beauty spot, and is also home to a classic example of a traditional lighthouse.

The little sandstone island is linked to the mainland by a tidal causeway.

Small in size, it has a rich history that dates back long before the lighthouse was built in 1898, to replace the one on the headland at Tynemouth Castle to the south.

The little island is thought to have been the home of hermits in the early days of Christianity, prior to the Viking invasion of 800, and the monks associated with the priory of Tynemouth built a chapel dedicated to St Helen there around 1090. This

St Mary's island and lighthouse at low tide.
NORTH TYNESIDE COUNCIL

chapel was said to have had a tower where a lantern was kept burning to warn ships about the rocks below, starting a great tradition of lighthouses on the island.

In centuries before 'modern' lighthouses were built, there are many reported examples of lights being displayed from church or abbey towers by clerics, as a benevolent aid to passing seamen.

After the Dissolution of the Monasteries, the island became owned by Queen Elizabeth I's surveyor for Northumberland, Thomas Bates, and was known as Bates Island. The current OS map has it as 'Bait Island' because the original mapmakers thought the name came from bait dug up by fishermen.

The deep channel in rocks on the north side is known as Smugglers Creek, and in 1722 Surveyor of Customs Anthony Mitchell was found dead nearby, thought to have been murdered by brandy runners.

Michael Curry, a worker at the Royal Sovereign Glass Works in Seaton Sluice, was executed in 1739 for killing Robert Shevil, landlord of the inn at Old Hartley, and his body hung from a gibbet at the landward end of the tidal causeway, at what is known today as Curry's Point. A plaque was unveiled there in 1989 to mark the 250th anniversary.

St Mary's was used in 1799 as a cholera isolation hospital for Russian soldiers en route to fight Napoleon, and those who died were buried there.

In 1855, fisherman and publican George Ewen built a cottage on the island and in 1862 turned it into a pub with water piped from a stream on the headland. A skeleton found on site, maybe that of one of the Russians, was kept in the cellar and visitors were charged to see it.

Ewen was evicted by Lord Hastings, the landlord, in 1895 in a dispute over the ownership of the cottage, and following complaints about rowdy customers trespassing on nearby land. He was replaced by tenant John Crisp, who turned it into a temperance hotel.

Following centuries of shipwrecks on St Mary's Island prior to that of the *Gothenburg* City from Montreal in thick fog in June 1891, when no lives were lost, the 125ft white-painted brick

From the late 19th century onwards, the impact of the decline of local coalmining and industry was lessened and ameliorated by the emergence of Whitley Bay as a seaside resort. The opening of the North Tyne Loop railway line in 1882, linking the coastal villages to Newcastle, generated tourist traffic to Whitley Bay, and several attractive railway publicity posters were produced in a bid to entice visitors from further afield, with St Mary's lighthouse as the centrepiece. The line, which included a new station in the centre of Whitley Bay, followed the route of the present Metro.
NATIONAL RAILWAY MUSEUM

covered with cement render lighthouse tower was built there in 1898 by the John Livingstone Miller company of Tynemouth using 645 blocks of stone and 750,000 bricks. A total of 137 steps lead from the ground floor to the lantern, which offers sweeping views of the North Sea.

The stone keeper's cottage next door is linked to the lighthouse tower by a covered passage.

Initially lit by paraffin vapour, the lighthouse, which had a range of 17 miles, was not converted to electrical operation until 1977, even though a mains supply had been supplied to the island in 1957.

Prior to the construction of the first causeway in 1929, low-tide access to the lighthouse was by stepping stones. The causeway was renewed in 1966.

The lighthouse became a trademark for the area, appearing on numerous publicity posters for the seaside resort of Whitley Bay over the decades, and became a favourite subject for paintings and postcards.

The causeway leading to St Mary's Island. GLEN BOWMAN*

In May 2012, the lighthouse was afforded Grade II listed status.

The site attracts up to 80,000 visitors each year, with around 14,000 climbing the steps to the top of the lighthouse. It also offers activities and events throughout the year, including education sessions to more than 4,500 local children.

The tower is open to guided tours at low tide daily from May to November and on weekends and school holidays from November to March. The site may be closed due to weather or tidal conditions.

The surrounding nature reserve contains an area of rockpools, clifftop grassland, a beach and newly created wetland habitats. The wetland is considered very important as a high-tide roost for golden plover, oystercatcher, curlew and redshank, and as a key landfall for passing migrating birds in spring and autumn.

A wineglass engraved to celebrate the completion of the lighthouse on St Mary's Island is displayed inside the National Maritime Museum at Greenwich. It is inscribed 'New lighthouse on St Mary's isle first used 1896.' ROBIN JONES

The lighthouse was automated in 1982 and declared redundant just two years later, superseded by modern navigational methods. The original Fresnel lens was sent to the now-closed lighthouse museum in Penzance with the current lens transferred from Withernsea lighthouse.

After it was decommissioned, the lighthouse was reopened as a visitor centre by North Tyneside Council, which in 2007 announced a £130,000 scheme to repair and repaint the tower. The Friends of St Mary's Lighthouse was set up to help preserve it.

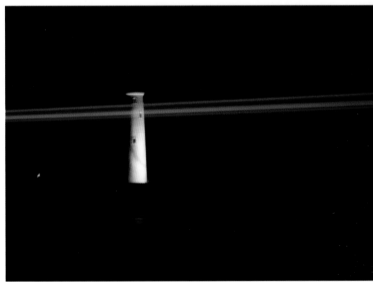

It's a lighthouse, but not as we know it! St Mary's lighthouse found itself illuminated by a rainbow laser during the build-up to the London Oylmpic Games in 2012. Global Rainbow, a £50,000 artwork created by American artist Yvette Mattern, lit up the skies over Tyneside from 29 February to 4 March that year. GLEN BOWMAN*

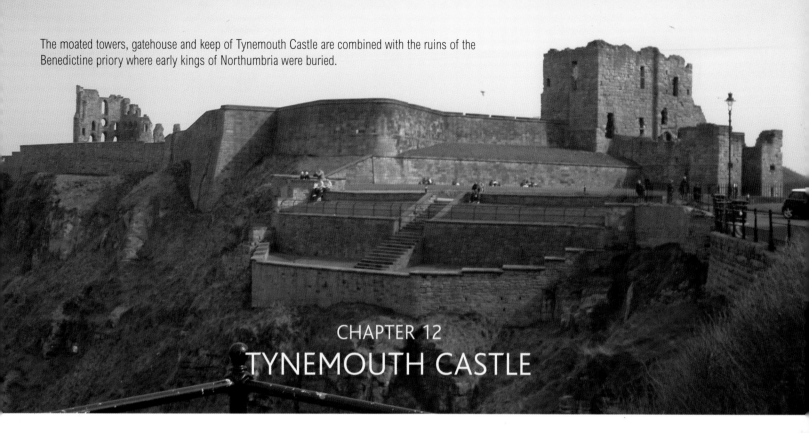

The moated towers, gatehouse and keep of Tynemouth Castle are combined with the ruins of the Benedictine priory where early kings of Northumbria were buried.

CHAPTER 12
TYNEMOUTH CASTLE

A CLASSIC EXAMPLE of an ecclesiastical light was to be found at Tynemouth Castle and Priory, the ruins of which stand on the small rocky peninsula of Pen Bal Crag. Perched on top of a sheer cliff, they comprise one of the most prominent landmarks on England's east coast.

It was realised in medieval times that navigational aids at this point were vital. A major danger to shipping is presented by a sandbar across the mouth of the River Tyne, where the outward current of the river at ebb tide is met by the incoming sea.

When a hard easterly wind is combined with heavy seas, entering North Shields harbour becomes perilous. A loaded ship ran the risk of hitting the sandbar at such times, and if the rudder became damaged, risked being driven on to Herd Sand, the Black Middens or the rocks at the foot of the castle.

The Black Middens are rocks which are covered at high water and over the centuries have claimed numerous ships after they

had safely negotiated the river entrance. In 1864, the Middens claimed five ships in three days with many deaths, although the wrecks were only a few yards from the shore.

The priory on the headland dates from the early seventh century when it may have been founded by King Edwin of Northumbria.

The body of the murdered King of Deira, Oswin, was brought to Tynemouth for burial in 651. He was made a saint and his grave attracted pilgrims. He was the first of three kings to be buried on the site, the second, Osred of Northumbria, who was murdered in 792 after being deposed, and the third, Malcolm III of Scotland, who was killed at the Battle of Alnwick in 1093.

The priory was raided by Vikings in 800, 832, 865, 870 and 875, when it was destroyed leaving just the parish church of St Mary.

A hand-coloured postcard dated 1901, showing Tynemouth Castle with its lighthouse (left), and in the distance to the right, Tynemouth North Pier, with its original lighthouse and waves apparently surging through the storm breach as described in the next chapter. AUTHOR'S COLLECTION

A Victorian print of Tynemouth Castle with its lighthouse on the far right.

During the reign of Edward the Confessor, Earl Tostig turned the site into a fortress. He intended to restart the long-abandoned priory, but was killed at the Battle of Hastings in 1066 before he had chance to do so. The Earl of Northumberland, Robert de Mowbray, brought in monks from St Albans to refound a monastery in 1090.

The prior of Tynemouth was in 1296 granted royal permission to surround the monastery with walls of stone, 3,200ft in total length, and a century later, a gatehouse and barbican were added on the landward side of the castle. The site became somewhat of a hybrid of a military and ecclesiastical establishment.

Early records indicate that an ecclesiastical light was shone from a coal brazier on a turret of the priory church, as a guide to ships entering the Tyne.

The monastery was disbanded in 1538 and the lands seized by Henry VIII, who upgraded the castle fortifications.

After the Dissolution of the Monasteries, it was maintained by Henry, the 8th Earl of Northumberland, the captain of the castle from 1561-85, who was paid a toll of four pence for every English ship entering the river and a shilling for every foreign one.

After the restoration of Charles II, Colonel Sir Edward Villiers became the governor of the castle, and repaired the fortifications in 1663. Around this time, he also replaced the monastic lighthouse which had collapsed in 1659. His new 79ft lighthouse, built using stone taken from the ruins of the priory, was situated at the north eastern corner of the promontory, with an adjoining house for himself. The white-painted tower was square at the base for the first 26ft and then octagonal up to the top.

In 1775, the lighthouse was rebuilt. A lantern room was added in 1802 when the light was converted from a coal fire to a revolving light with silvered parabolic reflectors and Argand lamps.

The author Jane Harvey published a short poem about the priory, castle and lighthouse in 1830:

No air-built castles, and no fairy bowers,
But thou, fair Tynemouth, and thy well-known towers,
Now bid th' historic muse explore the maze
Of long past years, and tales of other days.
Pride of Northumbria!—from thy crowded port,
Where Europe's brave commercial sons resort,
Her boasted mines send forth their sable stores,
To buy the varied wealth of distant shores.
Here the tall lighthouse, bold in spiral height,
Glads with its welcome beam the seaman's sight.
Here, too, the firm redoubt, the rampart's length,
The death-fraught cannon, and the bastion's strength,
Hang frowning o'er the briny deep below,
To guard the coast against th' invading foe.
Here health salubrious spreads her balmy wings,
And woos the sufferer to her saline springs;
And, here the antiquarian strays around
The ruin'd abbey, and its sacred ground.

Under an Act of Parliament in 1836, Trinity House was allowed to compulsorily purchase private lighthouses, and bought the one at Tynemouth Castle from William Fowke in 1841 for of £124,678.

The light was improved again in 1871. Its revolving red light 154ft above sea level could be seen for 18 miles.

It was finally made redundant by the building of a more modern lighthouse on St Mary's Island, as described in the previous chapter. The light was discontinued from 31 August 1898, and the tower was demolished between November 1898 and January 1899. The governor's house was demolished in November 1902.

The castle returned to military use during World War Two when it was used to defend the mouth of the Tyne. A new coastguard station was opened by Prince Charles in 1980, but was closed in 2001.

The castle site is now managed by English Heritage which charges an admission fee.

A 19th-century illustration of a lifeboat rescuing survivors from a shipwreck with Tynemouth Castle and its lighthouse on the rocky headland of Pen Bal Crag in the background. The ship has struck upon the rocks at the foot of the cliff on which the lighthouse is built. In the 19th century, it was said that because of the danger of entering Shields harbour in stormy weather, with the wind from the eastward, more ships were wrecked there than at the entrance of any other harbour in Britain.

CHAPTER 13
TYNEMOUTH AND SOUTH SHIELDS

THE PHRASE taking coals to Newcastle was first recorded in 1538, but the Tyne had been a major sea port since Roman times.

Because it is situated next to major coalfields, the Tyne had been a major export route for the black stuff since the 13th century.

From 1530 onwards a royal Act restricted all shipments of coal out of Tyneside to Newcastle Quayside. The net result was to hand a monopoly in the coal trade to a cartel of Newcastle burgesses called the Hostmen. This monopoly helped Newcastle's growth into a major town.

It remained a major coal exporter until the decline of mining in the second half of the 20th century.

Massive wooden coal staiths for loading coal on to ships were located at Dunston in Gateshead, Hebburn and Tyne Dock in South Shields, where today, coal arrives in the opposite direction, with more than two million tons imported each year.

During the late 19th and early 20th centuries Tyneside was one of the world's most important centres of shipbuilding.

The river became a massive trade highway, and to improve navigation, its lower reaches were straightened out during Victorian times, with islands removed.

Most important of all was the entrance to the Tyne from the North Sea.

A lone seagull escapes the deluge by inches as a giant wave crashes over the end of North Pier obscuring the lighthouse. JULIE PEARSON

The North Pier takes another battering as it protects the entrance to the Tyne. JULIE PEARSON

The 1897 breach in the North Pier, with the original lighthouse getting a pounding from another wave at the end, is unmistakeable in this hand-coloured postcard sent in 1906, on the back of which the writer refers to "the damage that was done to Tynemouth Pier during a severe storm many years ago." AUTHOR'S COLLECTION

The mouth of the Tyne is naturally exposed to the full ravages of the ocean, and in rough weather ships were regularly wrecked.

In 1852, the Tyne Improvement Commission obtained an Act of Parliament to allow piers on both side of the river mouth to be built, affording protection to vessels.

In the early years of the 19th century, nine engineers presented blueprints for the north and south piers. The one which was selected came from James Walker, president of the Institution of Civil Engineers.

The foundation stones were laid in 1854, when work began on the North Pier, with the construction of the South Pier beginning two years later.

However, it took until 1895 to complete the piers, a project originally estimated to last seven years, because of the sheer

Tynemouth's North Pier lighthouse on a calm day. MICHAEL MARSTON*

difficulty in laying stones and working in what was often some of the most inhospitable of conditions anywhere on the English coast.

Lighthouses were added to the North Pier in 1864, in the form of a 55ft tower, and the South Pier in 1895.

The North Pier was breached in 1867 by a storm surge when it was being built. It was breached again in 1897, after which it took twelve years to repair the damage. Following the storm, which left the lighthouse isolated, with large sections of the walkway having completely disappeared, The remaining parts of the breakwater were found to be unstable and were rebuilt to a design by John Wolfe-Barry, who built Tower Bridge in London.

The North Pier lighthouse we see today was built by Trinity House in 1903, before the rest of the breakwater was completed. It was only on 15 January, 1908 that it was brought into use.

The North Pier, which lies in Tynemouth itself, is 2,950ft long and cost £1,544,000 to build including the reconstruction, while the South Pier, which adjoins South Shields, is 5,150ft long and cost £526,000. A distance of 1,181ft separates the round heads of both piers. More than three million tons of stone were used to build them.

Magnesium limestone quarried at the Tyne Commissioners' Trow Quarry a mile from the South Pier was used to build them, as well as the lower courses and facings of the piers themselves. The stone was cut into radial blocks at the South Pier block yard.

The tapered tower of North Pier lighthouse stands 75ft high, with a focal plane of 85ft, and its white light can be seen for 26 miles. The lantern rotates to give a group of three white flashes every ten seconds, and may have come from the original lighthouse. The foghorn mounted on the tower emits one blast every ten seconds.

The South Pier lighthouse is by comparison a stubby 39ft high, with the outside of the lantern room painted red on the Tyne-facing side and white on the sea-facing side.

It has a white light which can be seen for 13 miles, a red light for 9 miles and a green light for 8 miles. The purpose of the green sector is to warn ships about Bellhues Rock a mile to the north.

The South Pier lighthouse today, with weathervane on top. JASON MILLER*

An eight-second flash with a second period of darkness is emitted.

The light operates at night and also in the daytime if a ship is due. A fog bell on the gallery is struck once every ten seconds in patchy visibility.

A third lighthouse near the mouth of the river, also operated by the Port of Tyne Authority, is that at Herd Groyne in South Shields.

In the 17th century, the south side of the river hereabouts was marked by a pair of beacons on the high ground known as The Lawe which overlooks the mouth of the river. In 1832, they were replaced by a pair of stone obelisks, East and West Lawe beacons, which cost £60 to build, each having a stone base, brick upper part and stone cap. Intended as daymarks, by lining up the pair, a safe passage into the river was indicated.

The building of the South Pier changed the currents in the river mouth, leading to sand being brought in by the incoming tide. A groyne was erected in 1882 at the north end of Littlehaven beach to stop the displacement of material from the Tyneside beaches into the river channel.

Somewhat basic in comparison to those of the two piers, a 49ft painted lighthouse on skeletal iron legs with an octagonal corrugated iron lantern and watch room was placed on Herd Groyne that year. It did not need to be anywhere near as robust as the pier lighthouses, over which sea surges regularly break, as it was protected by the piers.

It is a pile lighthouse, that is, one built on stilt-like legs called piles – which could be screwed into the sandy base of the groyne for stability, rather than relying on traditional foundations. A staircase leads to the service room just below the lantern, while a ladder on the inside of the tower allows the keeper to climb up to the light itself.

Separate lanterns displayed lights both out to sea and up the river. The lighthouse has a focal plane of 49ft and its traditional light flashes eight seconds on, two seconds off, depending on direction, matching the light character of the South Pier lighthouse. The light is shown using a projector covered by coloured plastic filters, although it would have originally been lit using a Fresnel lens.

The fog bell on the gallery sounds once every ten seconds, automatically in poor weather.

All three of these lighthouses can be accessed on foot, but are not open to the public, and the piers are closed off in stormy weather. The Port of Tyne Authority now holds occasional heritage open days at the North Pier lighthouse.

Below: Herd Groyne lighthouse at South Shields, with the North and South piers and their lighthouses on the horizon. PAUL KING

Bottom: West and East Lawe beacons today. ANTHONY CURTIS*

CHAPTER 14
NORTH SHIELDS

SAFELY NAVIGATING a passage in and out of the mouth of the Tyne may have been the biggest problem facing mariners for centuries, but it was not the only one on the river.

At North Shields, just upstream from Tynemouth, a series of lights has been erected to mark the river channel, because of the difficulty of navigating ships past the treacherous Black Midden rocks.

In 1537, the Master and Brethren of Trinity House of Newcastle was granted permission by Henry VIII for a pair of tallow candle lights at North Shields. They were first marked graphically on Ralph Gardner's 1655 perspective map of the Tyne, but in 1727, a more substantial set was provided, on or near the same site.

They were built on and above what is now known as Fish Quay in the form of a High Light, the range, a white-painted four-storey square brick tower with a lantern at the top. It can be seen today at the junction of Beacon Street and Tyne Street.

Its corresponding Low Light, the range front, was 300 yards away on the waterside. The original lighthouse station was in 1672 enclosed by Clifford's Fort, a military installation and part of a chain of coastal defences against the Dutch. If not rebuilt in 1727, it is likely that the Low Light was extensively remodelled at this time, because the fort governor's new house built the year before was obstructing the light.

Once aligned when viewed from the sea, the pair indicated the safe channel. They used candles for illumination until 1773 when oil lamps were installed.

The problem with such pairs of lighthouses is that when the deepwater channel moves, they become redundant. The lights were duly discontinued for this reason in 1807.

An 85ft replacement for the Low Light was then designed by

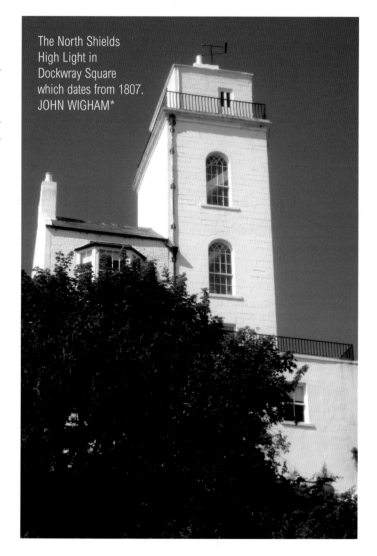

The North Shields High Light in Dockwray Square which dates from 1807. JOHN WIGHAM*

Robert Salmon's 1828 painting of the Low Light at North Shields. The Old Low Light which it replaced is the red building to the immediate right of the Flagpole.

John Stokoe for the local Trinity House. A square tower stone building, broadly similar in appearance to the Old High Light, with a small lantern on the roof, the New Low Light was 82ft above sea level and was visible for 13 miles.

Dockwray Square was chosen as the site for a replacement High Light, also built to a Stoke blueprint. Standing 58ft tall, and 138ft above sea level, the New High Light somewhat matched the appearance of its predecessor. Its fixed white light could be seen for 16 miles.

The lights in both new lighthouses were turned off in the late 1990s, at which time the buildings were sold for residential and other uses. At this time a directional light was installed in the Herd Groyne lighthouse described in the previous chapter.

Distinctive and very visible, the white buildings mark a safe and clear entrance to the Tyne, so in daylight they are still very much used as daymarks, aiding entry by the pilots and others.

Not so the Old Low Light, which survives in the Fish Quay Conservation Area in a form that does not resemble a lighthouse. Its rectilinear as opposed to narrow vertical tower form is certainly unusual in this field.

Grade II listed, it is the oldest surviving building on Fish Quay, an area which, appropriately, was originally known as Low Lights. Sometime after being declared redundant, the Old Low Light was turned into the Trinity Alms Houses and given a pitched roof. Its white gable was painted black and its light window blocked to obscure it as a navigational landmark.

The Old Low Light has also been used as a fish warehouse. In the 20th century the building became as a training establishment for the Deep Sea Fisheries Association and later the Maritime Volunteer Service, which left in 2011.

Owner North Tyneside Council has leased it to the Tyne and Wear Building Preservation Trust which is refurbishing it, and local firm, Ainsworth Spark Associates, was appointed to advise on architectural aspects of the internal building work required.

It is hoped to turn the three-storey structure into a visitor, cultural and heritage centre, with a café and gallery space downstairs and conference rooms and offices above. For this purpose, a £300,000 grant has been awarded from the Fish Quay Townscape Heritage Initiative Common Fund, which was set up by the Heritage Lottery Fund with the local council, which has restored Clifford's Fort.

The demolition of disused fish processing buildings inside the fort has opened up sweeping views from the Old Low Light across the mouth of the Tyne.

The other three lighthouses are also listed buildings.

Fish Quay itself dates back to c1225, when Prior Germanus

The New Low Light on Fish Quay illuminated at night.
PAUL STAINTHORP*

Port of Tyne Authority

NEW LOW LIGHT

The new Lighthouse and Keeper's
house were erected in 1808-10
by the Master and Brethren of
Trinity House, Newcastle,
to replace the Old Low Light.
It still serves as an
important navigational aid
to vessels entering
the river.

The blue plaque affixed
to the New Low Light.
JACOB BAX

The New Low Light of 1808 at
Fish Quay. JOHN WIGHAM*

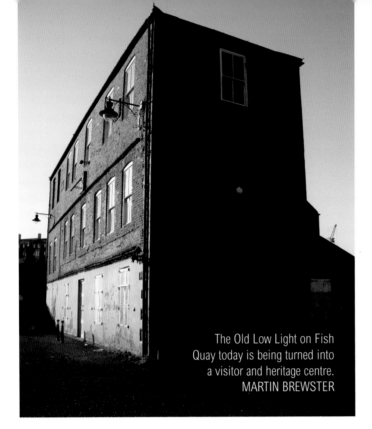

The Old Low Light on Fish Quay today is being turned into a visitor and heritage centre. MARTIN BREWSTER

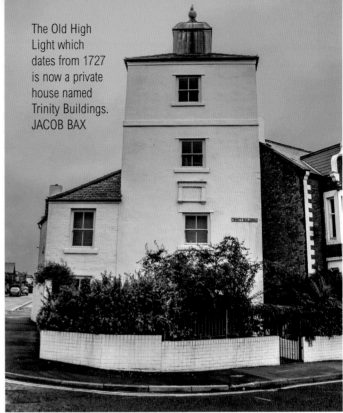

The Old High Light which dates from 1727 is now a private house named Trinity Buildings. JACOB BAX

A wintry day sees a ferry passing Fish Quay and the New Low Light, which still functions as a white-painted daymark. MICHAEL MARSTON*

A view of the arrangement of lighthouses at North Shields. The High and Low Lights are seen to the left, with the Old High Light further to the right of the newer High Light, and the Old Low Light covered in scaffolding. MICHAEL MARSTON*

from Tynemouth monastery, created a basic village of huts known as shielings at the mouth of the Pow Burn, hence the name Shields. Located to the east of the present Fish Quay, it expanded to include mills, bakehouses, a fish quay and brewery.

At first used by fisherman who supplied the priory, eventually other traders saw the benefit of a landing place situated so close to the river mouth, and by the end of the century, there were around 100 homes there, with a population of about 1000.

North Shields was, however, hindered in its development by the protective legislation which gave Newcastle a virtual monopoly over all seaborne trade apart from the loading and discharging of salt or fish.

The 'big cousin' upstream did everything in its power to stifle competition from its earliest days. In 1290 it was claimed that Fish Quay was "where no town ought to be" and was creating a loss for both Newcastle and the Crown. The Newcastle burghers petitioned King Edward I and managed to suspend trade from the new settlement.

The Fish Quay area became the core of historic North Shields and it expanded up the surrounding slopes. Wealthier residents built properties firstly in Dockwray Square (which had poor water supplies that later degenerated into slums), North-umberland Square and Howard Street, the present-day town centre.

The comedian Stan Laurel lived in Dockwray Square for several years before he achieved Hollywood stardom with Oliver Hardy: a statue of him stands there today.

CHAPTER 15
THE TYNE SWING BRIDGE

ONE OF THE most obscure surviving lighthouses is that positioned on the Tyne Swing Bridge, which links the centre of Newcastle-upon-Tyne with Gateshead.

The hydraulic swing bridge was built by the River Tyne Commission under powers conferred by the Tyne Improvement Act of 1861 and paid for by William Armstrong – the same who lived in Bamburgh Castle – so bigger ships could move up the Tyne to his company's Elswick Works.

It was in 1847 that he founded the Sir W.G. Armstrong and Company works to produce hydraulic machinery, cranes and bridges, soon to be followed by artillery, notably the Armstrong breech-loading gun, which re-equipped the British Army after the Crimean War.

The previous bridge on the site, a nine-arch stone structure which dated from 1781, was demolished in 1868. In turn, it had been built on the site of the Old Tyne Bridge of 1270, and most likely on that of the Roman bridge, Pons Aelius, which was constructed of wood and stone in c120 A.D. by the Emperor Hadrian and stood until 1248 when it burned down.

Building work on the Swing Bridge which was designed by John Ure began in 1873, and it was first used for road traffic on 15 June, 1876, with river traffic following on 17 July that year, when an Italian naval vessel, the *Europa*, became the first ship to pass through, on its way to Elswick Works.

The bridge has three masonry piers and a 281ft cantilevered span with a central axis of rotation which allows it to move through 360 degrees so that ships can pass on either side.

The hydraulic power still used to move the bridge is today derived from electrically driven pumps. These feed a hydraulic accumulator sunk into a 60ft shaft below the bridge. The water is then released under pressure which runs the machinery to turn the bridge.

The mechanism used today is still the same machinery originally installed by Armstrong. The finished bridge was hailed as an engineering triumph of Victorian Britain.

Installed in 1876 was a round lantern centred on an octagonal control room atop the arched bridge as a guide to navigation. The lantern is painted dark blue, while the control room is white with a dark blue roof.

Trade boomed after the Swing Bridge opened, making coal shipments from northwest Durham much easier, leading to the opening of new staithes at Dunston in 1893 and 1903. However, following the closure of the staithes firstly at West Dunston in 1934, Derwenthaugh in 1960 and finally Dunston in 1980, the openings became infrequent.

In 1972 the bridge was operated using a three-shift system by a team of 15 men under the control of the Master of the Bridge.

A heatwave could close the bridge when the metal expanded and 'welded' it to its mountings. In such cases, the fire brigade would be called to douse the bridge with water. From the 1960s, the bridge was painted in a light colour to reflect the heat.

The bridge today opens only around four times a week, compared to 6,000 swings in the peak year of 1924. It still provides a vital road crossing and is permanently manned.

However, the light has not been listed as an aid to navigation for many years.

In 1894, Elswick Works built and installed the steam-driven pumping engines, hydraulic accumulators and hydraulic pumping engines to operate London's Tower Bridge.

Three years later, the company merged with that of Armstrong's old rival, the late Joseph Whitworth, and became Sir W. G. Armstrong, Whitworth & Co Ltd. The firm not only built railway locomotives but armaments, ships, cars, trucks and aircraft.

After World War One, Armstrong Whitworth turned its Scotswood Works in Newcastle over to the production of railway locomotives. Its biggest contract was the building of 227 'Black Five' 4-6-0s for the London Midland & Scottish Railway in 1936 – the largest single locomotive order ever given by a British railway to an outside contractor. Nine Armstrong Whitworth 'Black Fives' have survived into preservation.

The navigational light that sits on top of the bridge. ROBIN JONES

Until the building of the Millennium Bridge, the Tyne Swing Bridge was the only one on the river that could move. ROBIN JONES

THE ATTRACTIVE red and white banded traditional lighthouse at Marsden near Whitburn has attracted generations of artists and photographers. However, its big claim to international fame was that it was the first lighthouse in the world designed specifically to use alternating electric current, state-of-the-art technology when it was built in 1871.

Occasionally referred to as Marsden lighthouse, it takes its official name from Souter Point a mile to the south, on which it was originally intended to build it. The lighthouse instead stands on Lizard Point, where the higher cliffs offer better visibility.

However, it kept the intended name of Souter lighthouse to avoid confusion with Lizard lighthouse in Cornwall.

Its main purpose was to reduce the number of wrecks on the underwater reef of Whitburn Steel which lies between the rivers Tyne and Wear.

The rocks had always been a nightmare for shipping and the situation worsened with the increase in coal and iron ore traffic following the Industrial Revolution. Furthermore, smoke pollution from industrial cities like Newcastle and Sunderland worsened visibility for mariners hugging this section of the Durham coastline.

It was rumoured that local people were involved in wrecking – setting up false lights to lure passing ships on to rocks so that they could steal their cargo when it washed ashore. However, local people particularly fisherman, also suffered at the hands of Whitburn Steel.

Wrecks were commonplace every winter during the 1860s.

Souter lighthouse, the first in the world to be powered by alternating current electricity, is now in the care of the National Trust.
GLENN SCOTT

On 24 November, 1865, the schooner *Test* hit the *Whitburn Steel* as it headed towards the Tyne. The crew was rescued by local fishermen manning the Whitburn lifeboat.

Captain Jerome Major said he had seen two bright lights in the sky and misidentified them as the Tynemouth lighthouses. He approached them, only to realise to his horror that he was heading to the shore and could not stop or turn round in time.

That December, local sea pilots and fishermen demanded an official investigation, a total of 17 ships having hit the reef since September 1964. The Board of Trade asked Trinity House in London to investigate and Rear Admiral Sir Richard Collinson led a commission which, during its visit to the locality, looked at a new gasworks and an optician's workshop whose windows faced the sea to the south and east as possible sources for the mystery lights, but ruled them out.

The Board of Trade enquiry opened in Sunderland's Custom House on 28 December, and heard statements from several witnesses who had seen mysterious lights in hazy or foggy weather, with similar reports dating back thirty years. The enquiry concluded that there was no evidence to suggest that decoy lights had been shown maliciously, but the source of the reported lights remained a mystery. The Tyne Pilotage Board was asked to carry out more investigations,

In November 1866, the South Shields bark *Margaret and Jane* hit the rocks in fog, its eight-man crew rescued by lifeboat, after the captain had turned towards what he wrongly believed to be the light from Tynemouth Castle lighthouse.

At a court of inquiry in 1867, local sea pilots claimed to have seen "a glare or reflection of a lofty light at the entrance to the Tyne" at certain states of the atmosphere over of Souter Point. While it would not fool an experienced crew with local knowledge, it was a clear hazard to outsiders. A special report was duly submitted to the Board of Trade.

Whitburn fishermen, angered at further suggestions that they were behind the mysterious lights, retorted that old colliers which were no longer seaworthy were being deliberately sent out by their owners with the hope of claiming on insurance, and that

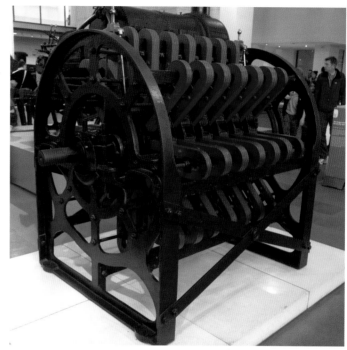

One of the groundbreaking generators from Souter lighthouse is preserved in the Science Museum. ROBIN JONES

The lantern gallery at the top of Souter lighthouse. EUGENE REGIS*

the false lights were an excuse given by their captains.

The controversy reached the pages of *The Times*, which said it was unbelievable that wreckers were responsible, as it was a crime previously unheard of on the North East coast, and that the government should step up its efforts to find the source of the lights. Its editorial added: "If these lights have been exhibited accidentally a proper light should be put up at once on Souter Point about which there could be no mistake."

While the debate raged on, 20 more ships were wrecked in 1869, and the fishermen raised a petition.

Eventually, Trinity House bowed to public pressure and agreed to build a lighthouse.

Therefore, Souter has another claim to uniqueness, as the only lighthouse at least in Britain that was built to eliminate a hazard caused by unexplained phenomena in the sky.

Please don't mention UFOs at this point! The exact cause of the aerial lights was never established, but it has been conjectured that they were an example of "will-o'-the-wisp" lights seen over bogland, as a result of the combustion of methane gas. Descriptions of such phenomena are similar to those of the lights which lured ships on to Whitburn Steel.

Souter lighthouse with its 77ft brick tower was designed and built for Trinity House by civil engineer Sir James Nicholas Douglass, FRS, (16 October,1826 – 19 June, 1898, who was knighted for building the fourth Eddystone lighthouse. He also worked on the Bishop's rock lighthouse off Land's End, working alongside his brother William as assistant to their father Nicholas, and after designing and building the Smalls lighthouse in Pembrokeshire, he completed another 19 for Trinity House, where he became engineer-in-chief in 1862.

The £8,000 contract for building the lighthouse and keeper's cottage was in 1869 awarded to the local firm of James Todd. The foundation stone was ceremonially laid by Admiral Collinson's sister on 9 June 1869.

Trinity House had been carrying out an exhaustive testing and selection process to find a better form of illumination. Electrical equipment in Britain and France was compared with oil lighting until alternating electric current-powered carbon arc lights were chosen, with Souter as the first lighthouse to use it. Carbon arc lights for lighthouses were pioneered by Professor Frederick Hales Holmes who had carried out experiments in 1857 at Blackwell and South Foreland off the Kent coast and a test installation at Dungeness in 1862. The first complete installation of this system was at Souter in 1870, with electricity provided by Holmes' own magneto electric generators for which he took out a series of patents. One of the Holmes generators built in 1867 and used at Souter is displayed in the Science Museum, London

Holmes' lights were magnified 230 times by a lens array in a rotating octagonal drum. The 800,000 candle power light could be seen for up to 26 miles.

Built 1,036ft from the cliff edge, Souter was brought on line in January 1891. As well as the revolving beacon light visible from the sea, a series of prisms reflected a red beam inland over Sunderland Bay, so that ships sailing too close to the coast were alerted to the dangers. When the flashing red beacon changed to white, it indicated that such vessels had steered towards safer waters. The lighthouse also had a foghorn.

The attendant buildings including the keepers' cottages were built in a square courtyard which also contained an engine house and workshop. At one stage, 30 people including the families of four keepers lived on the premises.

Tanks with a 60,000-gallon capacity were built below the courtyard, to collect rainwater for feeding the boilers of the engines which powered the generators and an air pump to feed the pressure tank of the foghorn.

As first built, a single foghorn of a clay and iron pipe design was installed. It was superseded in 1873 by a pair of twin horns to the same design, angled to spread the noise up and down the coast.

These were replaced by twin Rayleigh trumpets in the 1920s, with the foghorn house remodelled at the seaward corners to accommodate them. In 1953, the present diaphone fog horns were installed.

The foghorn emitted a five-second blast every thirty seconds in poor weather. It had a siren signal of a five-second burst of

480 Hz every five minutes.

Douglass became a Fellow of the Royal Society in 1887 and retired from Trinity House five years later. He died at his home on the Isle of Wight in 1898. His youngest son Alfred trained as a lighthouse engineer. His eldest surviving son William Tregarthen Douglass also made a reputation for himself in lighthouse building.

Unlike most other Trinity House lighthouses, Souter was never automated, and few alterations were made, a notable exception being the conversion of the light from electricity to oil in 1914, when a bigger lantern was installed. Souter was electrified once again in 1952, but this time, the power came from the mains supply.

As a result of few changes apart from those made to its lantern and electrical apparatus, Souter stands today as a near as possible example of a lighthouse in its original form.

Improvements in navigation made Souter redundant, like so many other lighthouses around the coast of Britain. It was decommissioned in 1988, but continued to serve as a radio navigation beacon until 1999 when it was finally closed.

The lighthouse and its surrounding complex, which are accessed from Coast Road in Whitburn, came into the care of the National Trust, which opens it to the public, who can inspect the engine room, tower and living quarters, and offer guided tours on certain days. Two of the keepers' cottages are used as National Trust holiday cottages throughout the year. Souter is one of the most visited lighthouses on this stretch of the coast.

The foghorns are sounded on special occasions, including the monthly Engine Room Day, which is held at the lighthouse during the summer months.

Souter is said to be haunted, and has even featured on TV's *Most Haunted* ghost-hunting programme.

The exterior of the tower was restored at a cost of £65,000 as a project in autumn 2013.

Lifeboat Day: Souter lighthouse was also built as a lifesaver following a huge number of shipwrecks in the 1860s which made this section of coast the most dangerous in England. JULIE PEARSON

CHAPTER 17
SUNDERLAND

THE MOUTH OF the River Wear has from earliest times offered a haven for ships, but not necessarily a safe one. Shifting sandbanks tended to collect at the point where the river diverges into various channels to enter the sea, and the easiest way of preventing it from building up to the point where it becomes a danger to shipping is to build piers either side of the river mouth.

The effect is to narrow the channel of water and deepen it, increasing its velocity at ebb tide. The result is the scouring of the harbour entrance and the removal of sand particles before they have time to settle.

Since at least 1200 and probably before, the harbour at the mouth of the Wear appears to have been known as Sunderland. The first Borough of Sunderland was created by a charter granted by Bishop Hugh du Puiset in 1183.

Over the centuries, Sunderland's harbour grew in stature, trading in coal and salt, and today is the UK's second largest municipally-owned port.

Once hailed as the biggest shipbuilding town in the world, vessels were built on the Wear from at least 1346 onwards. By the middle of the 18th century, Sunderland was one of the chief shipbuilding towns in Britain. However, overseas competition caused a downturn in demand for Sunderland-built vessels and the last shipyard in the port closed on 7 December, 1988.

In 1669, Charles II authorised Edward Andrew to build a pier, erect lighthouses, and cleanse the harbour at Sunderland, raising the necessary funds by imposing a tonnage duty on ships. Major improvements to the harbour and port were undertaken soon after the River Wear Commission, an elected committee of local colliery owners, landowners, merchants and ship owners, was formed in 1717. The commission controlled and financed the

The original stone lighthouse on Sunderland's Old South Pier as depicted in *The Ports, Harbours, Watering-Places, and Picturesque Scenery of Great Britain*, illustrated by views taken on the spot, by William Finden, William Henry Bartlett and William Andrew, published in 1840. The old North Pier light is in the background. The large D on the fore topsail of the collier is a distinguishing mark adopted by the owner so that his ships may be readily identified.

An Edwardian postcard of Sunderland's Roker lighthouse, with its red and white bands created by building it from naturally-coloured Aberdeen granite. AUTHOR'S COLLECTION

A late 1930s' hand-coloured postcard of Roker Sands with the lighthouse and pier in the background. AUTHOR'S COLLECTION

The lighthouses on the Old North and South piers stand sentinel over the entrance to Sunderland's harbour in 1883. AUTHOR'S COLLECTION

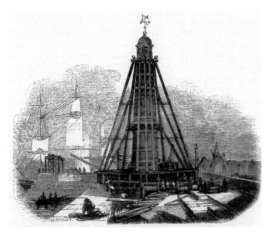

From left to right: A sketch of the moving of the Old North Pier lighthouse in 1840. AUTHOR'S COLLECTION; The blueprint for the shifting of the Old North Pier light in 1840. AUTHOR'S COLLECTION; The laying of the final stone of Roker lighthouse at the opening ceremony – engineer Henry Wake and the other dignitaries including the Lord Lieutenant of Durham, the Earl of Durham, are on the raised platform positioning the black marble stone above the door on 23 September, 1903. SUNDERLAND CITY COUNCIL

development of the docks and harbour, continually striving to change the shape of the river so as to open it up to more and bigger vessels.

Work on what is now referred to as the Old South Pier was started in 1723, in a bid to divert the river channel's current away from the sandbanks.

In 1748, a second breakwater, that is now known as the Old North Pier, was first proposed.

At first, piles were driven into the seabed and a line of old keelboats were sunk to form a temporary breakwater.

However, the building of a permanent stone structure began in 1786. Consisting of a wooden frame filled with stones, it protruded 1,500ft into the sea. It was then decided to face the framework with masonry.

A lighthouse with reflectors was built at the seaward end in 1794, shortly after which around 700 yards of the pier had been enclosed by masonry by the commission's engineer Robert Stout.

A stone lighthouse was built on the Old South Pier by Stout's successor Jonathan Pickernell in 1802. A tide light, which shone red, it was displayed only when there was sufficient depth of water on the bar for ships to enter the harbour. In the day, a flag was hoisted during tide time.

Pickernell also erected a new 75ft octagonal lighthouse tower on the Old North Pier in late 1802, when he extended its length by another 115ft. Shown from sunset to sunrise, it was visible 12 miles away in good weather.

The Old North Pier was extended to 1,770ft by the commission in 1840-1. In a remarkable operation by engineer John Murray, Pickernell's lighthouse was moved in one piece 450ft along the pier to its new end. The well-documented operation took place between 2 August and 4 October, 1841 and was undertaken using a timber cradle to support the 338-ton tower.

Resting on bearers, running on 250 6in diameter wheels, six railway tracks were laid to move the cradle, using three windlasses. Once positioned, the cradle was removed so that a new stone foundation could be built beneath the lighthouse.

Even more remarkable was the fact that not only did the

lighthouse remain undamaged during the operation, but its gas lamp was shone each night during the operation.

The Port of Sunderland was significantly expanded in the 1850s with the building of Hudson Dock to designs by the commission's engineer John Murray, with consultancy by railway engineer Robert Stephenson, he of *Rocket* fame. The original lighthouse on the Old South Pier was replaced in 1856 by a 50ft round cast iron tower with lantern and gallery painted white, designed by Thomas Meik.

It originally displayed three lights; one from its main lantern, a second from a smaller semi-circular window and the third from a normal flat window at the base of the tower. The back of the main lantern has a small circular window allowing for the operator to ensure that the light was lit, even from a distance. The light was visible for 10 miles.

By the end of the 19th century, the harbour had grown from

Thomas Meik's Old South Pier lighthouse of 1856 now stands in Roker Park, as a monument to Sunderland's seafaring and industrial heritage.
CHRIS PERRIMAN*

Now known as Beacon Lighthouse, the former Old South Pier Tower at Roker Park is illuminated at night as a landmark.
LIAM SWINNEY*

a small and treacherous natural inlet to one of the largest coal shipping ports in Britain. An estimated 15,000 tons of coal were transported each day.

Yet so much of the harbour had been ravaged by the elements over a century and needed to be both upgraded and replaced, despite the fact that the extension of the Old North Pier had created a fairly safe deepwater channel,

It was decided to create a new outer harbour, with two curving piers which would encompass the river mouth and the existing old harbour, and create 125 acres of protected water for shipping. The Old North Pier was superseded by Roker Pier, the northern arm of the outer harbour, with the foundation stone laid on 14 September, 1885. It was intended to turn Sunderland into 'the finest harbour of refuge on the east coast'.

Comprising granite-faced concrete blocks each weighing up to 45 tons, the new breakwater was built by the commission's chief engineer Henry Hay Wake, who faced numerous physical problems.

To extend the pier out to sea, massive foundations had to be sunk, and the sand covering the bedrock cleared. A special ship,

The restored lantern house at the top of Roker lighthouse.
SUNDERLAND CITY COUNCIL

The much-loved landmark of Sunderland's Roker lighthouse at dusk.
MARK WALKER*

the *Sandrail*, was built by Wake for this purpose. It was based around a huge suction pump which could shift 800 tons of sand each hour.

Once the sand was removed, a barge appropriately named *Concrete* and also designed by Wake arrived to deposit a pair of 56 or 116 ton bags of dry concrete on each trip. The concrete powder in the bags was dry, but once it reacted with the seawater, it solidified into position.

The blocks to make the pier were constructed on shore, at a spot which today is still known locally as the blockyard. Concrete was poured into huge wooden moulds and after setting, the blocks were hauled by a steam locomotive on a contractor's railway laid on the pier, to a radial crane

The vast crane called the *Goliath*, and set on a cradle, and both also designed and built by Wake, was driven by a pair of 20hp gas engines. The gas was supplied by pipes in a tunnel which ran the whole length of the new pier.

The pier, which cost £29,000 to build, grew to 2,000ft in length and had a new lighthouse on its head.

Roker lighthouse comprises a 75ft tapered round tower, built in bands of naturally-coloured red and white Aberdeen granite, but left unpainted. This was a new take on the old method of painting lighthouses in traditional red and white lighthouse stripes, but minus the long term costs of repainting and maintenance. Its lantern is painted white with a black dome.

The original lantern was gas powered and emitted a 45,000 candlepower reflected beam which could be seen for more than 15 miles out to sea. At the shore end were cottages for the keepers.

Built in 1902-3 by Wake, Roker has been described as

On 30 April, 2014, the Australian great-great-granddaughter of engineer Henry Hay Wake who built Roker Pier and lighthouse visited the landmark for the first time. Accompanied by her father Geoff (centre), Carmen Higgs (left) came face to face with initials carved into the tunnel beneath the pier 123 years ago to mark her great-grandfather's Mervyn's first visit there as a child in 1891 .

Engineer Henry Hay Wake had the initials of at least three of his children carved into the walls of the tunnel to mark their visits to the pier over a seven-year period between 1891-98. It is hoped that as work progresses more names will be uncovered. Carmen also met Sunderland born and bred Marilyn Stalton (right), another member of her extended family, who was shown the name of Henry's youngest child - her grandmother Enid - on another plaque. They were also shown inside Roker lighthouse's lantern house. The tour was arranged during Sunderland City Council's £1.35m restoration of the pier and lighthouse. SUNDERLAND CITY COUNCIL

The tunnel beneath Roker Pier leading to the lighthouse.
SUNDERLAND CITY COUNCIL

Britain's most powerful port lighthouse. Indeed, when completed on 23 September, 1903, the pier and lighthouse complex was hailed as a true "triumph of engineering."

The tunnel which had carried the gas pipes for the crane found a new lease of life, and was used by keepers to access the lighthouse in bad weather

The lighthouse was modernised in 1976 with the replacement of the original prismatic lens by sealed beam units, and again in 2007 when a low energy rotating lamp took their place.

The light has a focal plane of 82ft and emits a white flash every five seconds. It can be seen from 23 miles away. A fog signal sounds a siren blast every twenty seconds.

A new South Pier was also built, but never reached its intended length of 2,844ft. It was said that had the new South Pier been completed, it would have contained sufficient area to be claimed by the Royal Navy as a naval base. The commissioners therefore decided to leave it unfinished, it was reported.

The Old South Pier's 1856 lighthouse was switched off in 1903 when it was superseded by Roker lighthouse.

The building of the two new piers had a detrimental effect on the old ones, because of the knock-on effect of increased wave action against them. Cracks appeared in the roundhead of the Old North Pier and Pickernell's 1802 lighthouse began to tilt. The tower was dismantled in 1902 and replaced by a shorter but more robust stone version.

By 1958, the roundhead had become so unstable due to constant buffeting by north-easterly storms that the commission cut the pier back and demolished the lighthouse and replaced it with a yellow steel mast.

The River Wear Commission was superseded by the Port of Sunderland Authority in 1973. The authority now operates Roker lighthouse.

In 1983, the Old South Pier was also shortened, and Meik's lighthouse was removed. Rather than scrapping the tower, it was re-erected on a site overlooking the sea in Roker Cliff Park off Whitburn Road, where it is maintained as a much-loved local landmark by the City of Sunderland. It was replaced on the truncated pier by a 27ft red-painted mast displaying a red flashing light, visible for two miles.

Sunderland City Council in 2013 embarked on a major project to restore both the Grade II listed Roker pier and its lighthouse using Heritage Lottery Fund grant aid. After more than a century of use, the 'new' pier was looking as worn and jaded as its predecessor, the stub of which remains in the harbour.

Inside Roker lighthouse, many original features are preserved, including the tidal gauge, parquet flooring, wooden panelling and blue Stoke-on-Trent tiles. However, the interior was said to be in desperate need of conservation and restoration. A £2 million grant package from the Government's Coastal Communities Fund, added to £800,000 of matched funding from the council, including a £1.35 million rolling programme of restoration for the pier and lighthouse, with private sector investment used to convert the old keepers' cottages into a high quality café, which was announced in February 2013.

Work on the lantern house which began that summer included the refurbishment and redecoration of the steel and glazed structure including the upgrading of the navigation beacon and fog warning signal.

In September that year, the Lottery indicated initial support for the pier and lighthouse project, awarding the council £53,200 to develop an activity plan and conservation plan, carry out further design and interpretation work and draw up a management and maintenance plan, in support of a potential £500,000 award. The aim is not only to restore Roker lighthouse to its former glory but to also open the pier tunnel to visitors.

Sunderland Council cabinet secretary Mel Speding said: "The pier has protected the entrance to Sunderland harbour for more than 100 years, but it's taken a real pounding from the North Sea and it's essential we carry out this work now so it can be enjoyed by future generations."

CHAPTER 18
SEAHAM

SEAHAM WAS A small agricultural community where the major local landowners were the Milbanke family. On 2 January, 1815, Anne Isabella Milbanke married the poet Lord Byron at Seaham Hall.

In a letter to a friend, Byron wrote: *"Upon this dreary coast we have nothing but county meetings and shipwrecks; and I have this day dined upon fish, which probably dined upon the crews of several colliers lost in the late gales. But I saw the sea once more in all the glories of surf and foam."* Indeed, In 1824, 30 ships sunk off the coast.

Oblivious to the vast coal seams which lay beneath their land, the Milbankes sold out to Lord Charles Stewart, the 3rd Marquess of Londonderry, who in 1828 began building a new dock for the export of coal, with the first ships arriving in 1831. The harbour was literally hacked out of the limestone cliffs.

A temporary wooden lighthouse built north of the entrance to the dock to lead ships into the port burned down in 1835. As a replacement, engineer William Chapman built a 58ft stone tower at Red Acre Point, also referred to as Lighthouse Cliff, on the north side of the harbour. On the top was a white revolving light with a fixed red one below.

The first keeper was William Fairless, a former soldier who had fought with Lord Londonderry against Napoleon. A town grew up around the dock, taking the name Seaham Harbour to differentiate it from the village.

Seaham's coal exports ended in the early Nineties, but it is still very much a working port. ROBERTO STRAUSS*

THE OLD LIGHTHOUSE, SEAHAM HARBOUR.

Left: The lighthouse at Red acre point, towering above the network of railway lines which once served the coal port. AUTHOR'S COLLECTION

Below: Seaham's north breakwater lighthouse bears the brunt of heavy seas in November 2007. The vertical-boilered Head Wrightson steam locomotive on the harbour wall used to work there, and was brought back for a photographic session by owner and restorer Beamish Museum. PAUL JARMAN

The oil burning lamps set fire to the interior of the Red Acre lighthouse in 1856, and it took a year to repair.

In 1905, the light was switched off when the dock was extended and deepened on the orders of the 6th Marquess, because it could not cope with the massive volume of coal being exported. The alterations included the building of a new lighthouse at the end of the 1,400ft long north pier.

The Red Acre lighthouse was left in position as a landmark until 1940. It was then knocked down because of fears that it could be used by the Germans as a navigational aid by land or sea.

The 1905-built 33ft black and white banded cast-iron circular tower with lantern has a focal plane of 39ft and emits a 1.2 second green flash every ten seconds. In bad weather, it shows continuous green. The light is visible for 12 miles. A foghorn sounds a blast every thirty seconds. The gallery was removed in the 1960s.

The South Pier has a 22ft red mast with a fixed red light at the top and which can be seen for 5 miles, and the harbour also has a 15ft mast with another red light which can be seen for 2 miles.

The lights are all operated by the Port of Seaham, part of the Ports of Excellence group.

CHAPTER 19
HARTLEPOOL AND SEATON CAREW

The present lighthouse at the Heugh is operated by PD Teesport.
ROBIN JONES

THE ROCKY COASTLINE around Hartlepool has been the cause of many shipwrecks over the centuries. Legend, no more than that, has it that when a French vessel sank off the coastline during the Napoleonic Wars, a monkey wearing military uniform was washed ashore with the wreckage and found by local fishermen. They interrogated the monkey, who they believed to be a French spy, and after he did not answer their questions, they placed him on trial and hanged him. The monkey has since become a symbol of the town, and the mascot of Hartlepool United.

Hartlepool has been a major seaport virtually since King John granted it a charter in 1201. In the Middle Ages, its natural harbour was improved to serve as the official port of the County Palatine of Durham. The main trade was fishing, which made Hartlepool one of the most important ports on Britain's east coast. A pier was built in the 15th century.

A decline in the fishing trade saw the harbour fall into decay by the early 19th century, when it was still a small town of around 900 people, but it received a new lease of life in the wake of the Industrial Revolution. In 1823 the local council and Board of Trade decided that the town needed new industry, so the decision was made to propose a new railway to make Hartlepool a port for exporting coal from the Durham coalfield.

The council agreed the formation of the Hartlepool Dock and Railway Company to extend the existing port by developing new docks, and link to both local collieries and the developing railway network in the south. In 1839, the running of the company was taken over by Stockton-on-Tees solicitor Ralph Ward Jackson, who bought land to the south-west, and established West Hartlepool, building new docks on the southern side of the channel running below the headland, He proved so successful at

The Lighthouse Café at the Heugh was hit by a shell during the 16 December, 1914 bombardment, but the lighthouse behind remained unscathed.
AUTHOR'S COLLECTION

Far left: The first Heugh lighthouse, as sketched in 1847.
AUTHOR'S COLLECTION

Below: The 1847 lighthouse at the Heugh, which lasted until it was dismantled for military reasons in 1915.
AUTHOR'S COLLECTION

Although modern in appearance, the
Pilots Pier lighthouse dates from 1899.
ROBIN JONES

shipping coal from West Hartlepool through his West Hartlepool Dock and Railway Company that ships grew bigger and his new town outgrew the old one.

Of course, on such a treacherous coast, major new harbours with a vastly-increased volume of shipping needed new navigational aids.

In 1836, a lighthouse was installed on the end of the Old Pier or Pilots Pier which had been built on the west side of the old harbour entrance. It was replaced in 1899 by a 39ft square pyramidal wooden tower on a frame, which was moved in 1911 when the pier was extended.

It was later boarded over and painted white with two narrow horizontal red bands on each face, and a rotating radar antenna was fixed to the top of the lantern.

With a focal plane of 43ft, a white light flashes every three seconds over the entrance channel, and is otherwise green.

In early Victorian times, the light on the harbour pier was not considered adequate by local mariners, and a public meeting about the problem was held in 1844.

Trinity House ordered the harbour authorities to provide a better light, and so in 1846 one was built on the Heugh, a headland overlooking the old pier.

A 46ft tapered sandstone tower with a lantern on top, is believed to have been the first successful gaslit lighthouse in the world. Its fuel was natural gas from nearby coal mines, and shone for the first time on 1 October, 1847; its light was visible for 18 miles.

It met its demise during World War One.

At 8.03am 16 December, 1914, three German cruisers began shelling Hartlepool. Their aim was to lure out Royal Navy ships to be destroyed by the battleships of the German High Seas Fleet and destroyed.

However, it did not work, because the German battleships which should have been lying in wait had sailed back to port the previous night after encountering Royal Navy destroyers.

A total of 1,150 shells were fired at the town over nearly an hour by the three ships from Admiral von Hipper's High Seas

The former Seaton High Light tower now stands as a feature in Hartlepool Marina, without its lantern. ROBIN JONES

THIS TABLET MARKS THE PLACE
WHERE THE FIRST SHELL FROM THE
LEADING GERMAN BATTLE CRUISER
STRUCK AT 8·10 A.M. ON THE
16TH OF DECEMBER 1914
AND ALSO RECORDS THE PLACE WHERE
(DURING THE BOMBARDMENT)
THE FIRST SOLDIER WAS KILLED
ON BRITISH SOIL BY ENEMY ACTION
IN THE GREAT WAR 1914-1918

The plaque, a stone's throw from the lighthouse at the Heugh marking the spot where the first soldier was killed on British soil in World War One, by the German bombardment of 1916. Previously, there had not been a military casualty on British soil since the Jacobites had been defeated at the Battle of Culloden in 1746. ROBIN JONES

Scouting Force: the 28,100 ton battlecruiser *Seydlitz*, the 25,300 ton battlecruiser *Moltke* and the 17,250 ton armoured cruiser *Blucher*.

The heavy calibre shells fired at almost point-blank range hit the steelworks, railways, seven churches, five hotels and more than 300 homes. The gasworks exploded like a firework. Residents fled to the town's park to escape the shelling and falling masonry. A total of 102 people died including nine soldiers, seven sailors, 15 children and 467 wounded.

The coastal defences were puny by comparison, but the battery at the Heugh, a few yards from the lighthouse – where the first soldier to die on British soil in World War One was hit by a shell – had some success. Targeting the *Blucher*, its rounds destroyed the forebridge and some of her guns, while killing nine sailors.

The last shell was fired at 8.52am, after which the battlecruisers sailed off into the mist.

There had been a simultaneous deadly attack on Scarborough, described in Chapter 24, and later on Whitby.

The raids caused public outrage, with the Germans being described as "baby killers". Allied propaganda made the utmost of it, boosting recruitment campaigns. While war had been declared several months before, it was only through the attacks on the three northern towns that many British people woke up to the true horror of the threat they were facing.

During the Battle of Dogger Bank on 24 January 1915, the *Blucher* was sunk and *Seydlitz* barely escaped, but was heavily damaged.

The lighthouse at the Heugh was not damaged in the raid, but the nearby Lighthouse Café was hit.

However, in 1915, the lighthouse was dismantled, because it was clearly in the line of fire of guns at the Heugh battery, which had been used as a military coastal defence for centuries, and no

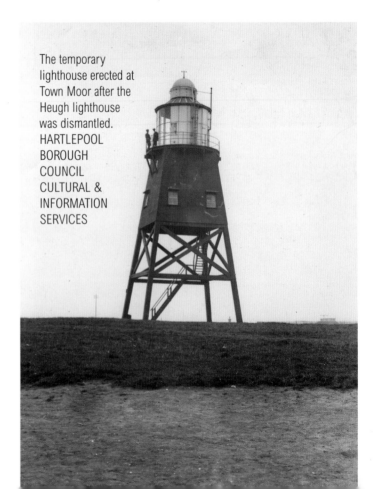

The temporary lighthouse erected at Town Moor after the Heugh lighthouse was dismantled. HARTLEPOOL BOROUGH COUNCIL CULTURAL & INFORMATION SERVICES

Above left: Seaton Carew's Low Light.

Above centre: At the end of a modern stone jetty opposite the Pilots Pier lighthouse is a set of six red and green lights to guide vessels into the marina and leisure complex which now occupies the Old Coal Dock. ROBIN JONES

Right: This post stands at the end of the outer North Pier which comprises the starboard light for entry into Hartlepool Marina. It is now solar powered. ROBIN JONES

chances were being taken in case the Germans should return. Its pioneering gas lamp and Fresnel lens are now exhibited in the Museum of Hartlepool.

It was replaced by a temporary light on nearby Town Moor, a wooden square pyramidal frame tower with enclosed watch room and lantern on top, sited behind the guns.

It was used until 1927, when a permanent replacement on the Heugh came into operation on 14 June. The 54ft white-painted round tower build from steel plates welded together with lantern and gallery was built near to the site of its predecessor, but gave a much better line of fire for the battery guns.

With a focal plane of 62ft, it emits two white flashes every ten seconds, day and night. Operated by PD Teesport, the light can be seen for 19 miles.

Now owned by PD Ports, Hartlepool's docks are still in use today and still capable of handling large vessels. However, a large portion of the former dockland was converted into a marina, capable of berthing 500 vessels, with a passage to and from the sea through a lock. Around the harbour are various navigational lights, including one fixed to the upper floor of the harbourmaster's office next to the entrance lock.

The story of Hartlepool's lights is inextricably linked with those of Seaton Carew, if only because one of them has been relocated to its big northern neighbour.

Two 70ft lighthouses were built there in 1838-9 to guide ships around the Long Scar Rocks a mile off the coast.

The round Seaton High Light was a Tuscan column built from ashlar sandstone around half a mile inland at the end of Windermere Road, reportedly 1,183 yards from the Low Light, a hexagonal tower which stood on what is now Coronation Drive just above the shore.

The High Light contained a newel helical stair lit by slit windows within the masonry. Keepers cottages were built alongside

The High Light, which was also known as the Longhill Lighthouse, displayed a fixed white light, and the low light was fixed red. To enter the Tees or Hartlepool harbour and miss the rocks, ships would line up the pair.

However, the channels changed as the seabed shifted, and after the South Gare light described in Chapter 21 became active in 1884, it superseded the Seaton Carew pair.

Nonetheless, the two continued in use until 1892 until the Tees Conservancy Commissioners turned them off. The Low Light may have been demolished around 1902 to clear the way for a tramway and road from Hartlepool.

The High Light remained in position, and eventually became enveloped by a tin recycling plant at the Longhill Industrial Estate and lost its gallery. Nonetheless, in 1985 it was given listed building status.

Two years after Hartlepool's coal docks were reopened as a marina in 1993, Teesside Development Corporation moved the High Light, now known as Seaton Tower, stone by stone to Jackson's Landing, where it was re-erected. In 1997 it was dedicated as a memorial to those who have lost their lives at sea.

There is also a navigational light attached to the front of the harbourmaster's office (blue building, right) next to the lock gates leading into Hartlepool Marina. JACQUELINE RAMSEY

CHAPTER 20
SEAL SANDS

SINCE THE Industrial Revolution, the River Tees has been used for transporting bulk goods, initially coal from the Durham mines and steel from the mills that developed around Middlesbrough.

As the original small docks in Yarm and Stockton-on-Tees became outmoded due to the growing size of ships, larger and deeper docks were developed, firstly in Middlesbrough and later further downstream at Teesport close to the mouth of the estuary.

In the 20th century, the Tees became important to the developing chemical industry. Teesport, which is owned by PD Ports, and lies on the south side of the estuary, is now the third largest port in Britain, handling over 56 million tonnes of domestic and international cargo each year.

Large scale chemical industries are based at Wilton on the south bank of the Tees and at Billingham and on recovered land at Seal Sands on the north bank.

In 1975, the Norsea Terminal, now known as the ConocoPhillips marine terminal, was built at Seal Sands.

The terminal is a crude oil reception, storage and trans-shipment installation. Its operations comprise

The front range light at the ConocoPhillips marine terminal dates from 1975 and is one of the most modern lights in this book.
AUTHOR'S COLLECTION

both processing and tanker loading facilities on a 307-acre site, with stabilised oil stored in a 375-acre tank farm at Greatham linked to the terminal by a 2-mile corridor containing pipelines, communications and utility services.

A pair of modern red-and-white hooped beacons were erected to mark the dredged channel into the new terminal. Oil tankers and other ships accessing the terminal line up the pair.

The front range light has four powerful red lights displayed through a window at the top.

The rear range light, which comprises a steel lattice structure, has six red lights arranged in a formation.

The lights come under the jurisdiction of the Tees and Hartlepool Port Authority.

The terminal has received numerous Gold Medals and President's awards from the Royal Society for the Prevention of Accidents over the years.

It stands on the edge of the estuary mudflats of Seal Sands, a 294.37 hectare biological Site of Special Scientific Interest, home to wildfowl and, as the name suggests, seal colonies.

The Teesside terminal is accredited to ISO 14001, the international environmental management system standard, which it has held continuously since October 1998.

The rear range light at the oil terminal.
AUTHOR'S COLLECTION

CHAPTER 21
SOUTH GARE AND REDCAR

THE BREAKWATER known as South Gare at the southern entrance to the Tees estuary comprises five million tons of slag from local blast furnaces.

It was built between 1861-84, with the slag given free by Tees-side blast furnace owners, who also paid for it to be moved.

The breakwater aimed not only to create a safe harbour for ships in stormy weather but facilitate the dredging of the river mouth.

It was a jewel in the crown of a wider land reclamation scheme which involved building 22 miles of training walls using blocks cast from the slag, an operation which was started in 1859. Effectively canalising the mouth of the Tees, the walls speeded up

William Henry Smith, son of the founder of the bookseller and newsagent, who officially opened South Gare breakwater in 1884. AUTHOR'S COLLECTION

the flow or water and slowed down the deposition of particles, keeping the deep-water channels free.

Before South Gare was built, dry land ended at Tod Point, with Coatham Sands and the mudflats of Bran Sands dividing it from the sea at low tide. The land was extended a further 2½ miles by the building of South Gare and backfilling the reclaimed muddy land with 70,000 tons of material dredged from the river bed.

Once the breakwater was complete, a pierhead was built at the north end using blocks of concrete weighing from 40 up to 300 tons.

On this pierhead, 5 miles north west of Redcar, a lighthouse was built in 1884. The 43ft white cylindrical cast-iron-clad stone tower has small porthole windows in the north and south side of the column to illuminate the internal helical newel staircase.

The building of the breakwater was overseen by John Fowler, engineer to the Tees Commissioners, and formally opened by William Henry Smith (1825–1891), First Lord of the Treasury, on 25 October, 1888. He is far better known today as a

An Edwardian hand-coloured view of South Gare breakwater and lighthouse, looking eastwards. AUTHOR'S COLLECTION

South Gare lighthouse with the coastguard station
and its navigational lights in the same compound.
JACOB BAX

newsagent who expanded his family firm of W. H. Smith, founded by his father, also William Henry Smith, (1792-1865) by selling books and newspapers at railway stations. He also became Leader of the House of Commons.

A railway was laid to carry men and materials from the Warrenby iron works to the South Gare construction site. After the breakwater was complete, it was used to move visitors, servicemen, lifeboatmen and lighthouse crew out to the lighthouse and army gun installations at a coastal battery built in 1891 at the south end as part of the Palmerston defence programme. What was unusual about this railway, and another that we will encounter in Chapter 28, was that it was wind powered. A sail was attached to a flat truck or bogie, and hauled the short trains in yacht fashion using the prevailing wind.

The track can still be seen in places along the breakwater.

The purpose of the South Gare light is to guide ships clear of Coatham Rocks off Redcar towards the Fairway Buoy in Tees Bay outside the bar at the estuary mouth. The same role was also being performed by the two lights at Seaton Carew and Hartlepool lighthouse.

As we saw, the Tees Conservancy Commissioners turned off the Seaton Carew lights in 1892.

South Gare and its breakwater take the full force of yet another surge. RED ROSE EXILE*

South Gare lighthouse viewed from the west, with a channel marker buoy in the foreground. RED ROSE EXILE*

The South Gare light has a focal plane of 53ft above mean high water. At first lit by a paraffin wick and later by pressurised paraffin burner, it was electrified in 1955. A mains-powered 500 watt tungsten filament incandescent light bulb with a backup bulb on the bulb changer operated with a backup diesel generator.

The lens rotation mechanism was originally powered by a clockwork motor but this was replaced by one duty motor and a backup motor.

The light source is held in an eight-windowed lantern housing under a hemispherical copper-domed roof. Below the windows there is a railed circular platform supported by brackets.

The light today is a 35 watt CDM-T lamp with a fourth order prismatic lens and is visible for 20 miles. In what in 2007 was a

South Gare lighthouse as viewed from the sea, with the lights on the coastguard station tower visible. RED ROSE EXILE*

The rear range light near the top of the Marks & Spencer grocery store in Redcar's Esplanade.

British and possibly world first, it is powered by a Schlunk 100 watt water-cooled hydrogen fuel cell. This system is more reliable than the mains electricity supply along the exposed breakwater which takes a pounding in stormy weather.

Still using the original lenses, the light is automatic, showing red and white sectors with a half-second flash every twelve seconds with an effective intensity of 150,000 candelas.

A fog signal was mounted to the west of the lighthouse but was later removed, as were the chimney and weather vane around 1980.

Operated by PD Ports, the lighthouse is a Grade II listed building and also has a code, ENG-131, given by the Amateur Radio Lighthouse Society: it can give status broadcasts using radio telemetry with the call sign G0SBN/P. The society was founded in 2000 and specialises in maritime communications, amateur radio, lighthouses and lightships. Its members travel to lighthouses around the world where they operate amateur radio equipment at or near the light.

South Gare lighthouse is off limits to the public and is ringed by a security fence, although the breakwter is accessible.

To the south of the lighthouse is a coastguard station with a short steel frame tower carrying a radar antenna, an automatic fog detector and a vertical set of four sectored red and white leading lights for navigation purposes. A second fog detector system is mounted on the Fairway Buoy.

A boathouse and slipway for the Teesmouth lifeboat station were built here in 1914, but in the 21st century its role was taken over by the Hartlepool lifeboat.

Redcar has a pair of small range lights on its promenade. The range rear light is a small appliance mounted on no less than the front of the two-storey red-brick Marks & Spencer store on the Esplanade.

With a focal plane of 36ft, it displays a red light, one-and-a-half seconds on, one second off.

The matching range front light is fixed on a pole across the street.

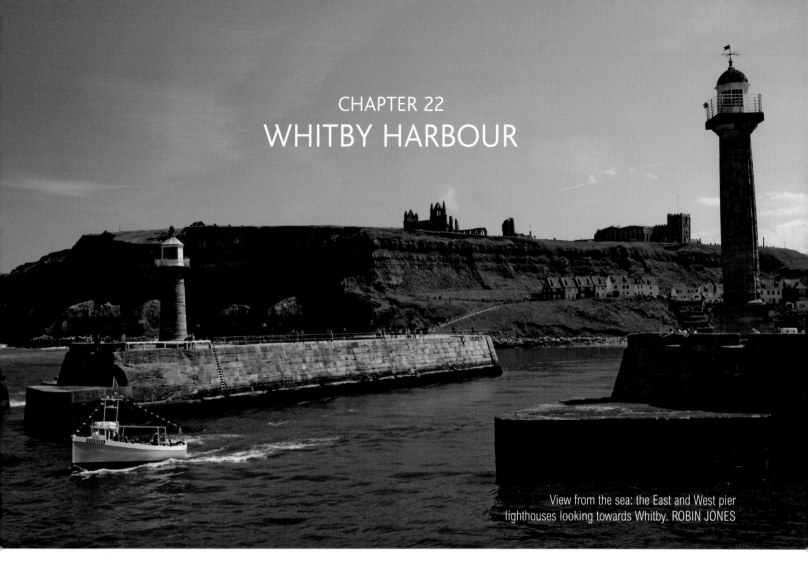

CHAPTER 22
WHITBY HARBOUR

View from the sea: the East and West pier lighthouses looking towards Whitby. ROBIN JONES

THE PORT OF WHITBY where the River Esk completes its journey from the moors to the sea is one of the real jewels on the coast of North East England. The town is famous for its association with Captain James Cook (1728-1779) the British explorer, navigator, cartographer, and Royal Navy captain who made the first recorded European contact with the eastern coastline of Australia and the Hawaiian Islands, and the first recorded circumnavigation of New Zealand.

As a teenager, he became apprenticed to Whitby ship owners and Quakers John and Henry Walker, who were in the coal trade. Their house is now the Captain Cook Memorial Museum.

A replica of his ship, the barque *Endeavour*, plies in and out of the harbour on short pleasure trips on a daily basis.

Whitby's top attraction is its ruined clifftop Benedictine abbey, where the future of Christianity in Britain was shaped. It was the setting in 664 for the Synod of Whitby, at which King

The replica of Captain Cook's ship the barque *Endeavour* passes the East Pier outer lighthouse while returning to the harbour. ROBIN JONES

Oswiu of Northumbria ruled that his church would adopt the Roman calculation of Easter, thereby severing ties with Celtic practices.

However, a close second has to be its magnificent harbour, its twin piers built to protect its once-great fishing fleet, which has four lighthouses.

The first pier known to have been built in Whitby was the Burgess or Tate Hill pier, which dates from 1190. It was repaired several times during the 16th century. Such early piers were built from timber.

In 1632 the Lord of the Manor, Sir Hugh Cholmley, began raising funds for a pier on the west side of the town, and a pier around 200 yards long appeared by the 1660s, maybe opposite the Burgess Pier, but details remain sketchy.

However, in 1702, an Act of Parliament was granted for the current East and West Piers to be built from stone.

The pair were shorter, lower and narrower than today. The West Pier was extended by 100 yards in 1735 when gun batteries

This modern rear range light is fixed to a lamp-post on the 199 steps below Whitby church.
ROBIN JONES

were installed on both sides of the harbour as coastal defences. The pier had a hexagonal lighthouse, with the light provided by three candles and a reflector.

After 1789, both piers were widened, lengthened and repaired, with around 75,000 tons of sandstone blocks used. Most of the work was done by 1814, with tolls from passing ships used to pay for the improvements.

A new sandstone lighthouse replaced the previous one on the West Pier in 1831, and was designed by Francis Pickernell, engineer to the harbour trustees. Its unpainted 83ft cylindrical fluted stone tower with white-painted lantern, black dome and gallery is mounted on a square base. The light could be seen for 10 miles.

The East Pier received its first lighthouse in 1855, a 55ft unpainted fluted Aislaby sandstone tower with a white-painted hexagonal lantern. Its green fixed light, with a red sector showing when the vessel entering the harbour is on an unsafe course up the wrong channel, could be seen 8 miles out to sea.

Between 1909-14, both piers had 500ft extensions added, in a bid to both increase shelter and reduce the amount of sand deposited at the previous harbour entrance. This move was considered important in view of the fact that from 1908, bigger ships could enter Whitby because the swing bridge which separates the upper and lower harbours had been built.

These extensions were constructed using a principle known as a "walking man", by which a steel framework inched its way forward along the seabed as required.

Once the piers were extended, new modern harbour lights were installed at the end of each.

On the West Pier extension, a 23ft green round wood lantern mounted on a square wood skeletal tower with unpainted wooden legs was erected in 1914. With a focal plane of 46ft, and automated, it shows a continuous green light. A foghorn on the end of the west extension sounds a blast every thirty seconds.

A new lighthouse on the East Pier extension, which also dates from 1914, is a red-painted version, also 23ft tall, with the lantern painted red. Also having a focal plane of 46ft, and also

The plaque attached to the West Pier light to mark its construction by Francis Pickernell. ROBIN JONES

This copper lantern served as the harbour light on the west pier until October 5, 1831, when it was replaced by the present lighthouse. It is now on display in the excellent Whitby Museum, which has a marvellous and exhaustive display of items from the town's proud seafaring past. ROBIN JONES

The newer and outer West Pier light. ROBIN JONES

A 21st century solar harbour light on the east harbour wall. ROBIN JONES

The West Pier lighthouse as seen from the doorway of its East Pier counterpart. ROBIN JONES

automated, it shows a continuous red light.

Although largely superseded by the 1914 lights at the end of the extensions, the West Pier stone lighthouse is still in use. With a focal plane of 79ft it displays a green light, flashing green twice in four seconds. It can be seen for 5 miles.

On the old East Pier lighthouse, although the conventional lantern has long since been disused, a red harbour navigation light is fixed to the top. Visible for 5 miles, it flashes twice every four seconds and has a focal plane of 40ft.

This light has largely been superseded by the placing of a

The East Pier lighthouse dates from 1855, but has not been used since 1914. ROBIN JONES

The West Pier lighthouse was built in 1831. ROBIN JONES

harbour light on the famous 199 steps leading from the east side of the port to the church and abbey, and which were immortalised in Bram Stoker's novel *Dracula*. It is attached to a traditional street lamp-post. The yellow light flashes every four seconds and has a focal plane of 150ft.

Since the navigational lights were modernised in 2012, a solar powered light on a steel metal post was erected on the harbour wall near the East Pier lighthouse. It emits a "quick flash" yellow light.

The lights are operated by the Port of Whitby.

The East Pier extension was closed to visitors several years ago, because the bridge linking it to the original structure began to crumble and so it was removed. You can still, however, walk the full length of the West Pier to the 1914 light at the far end.

In February 2012, the West Pier lighthouse was closed to visitors, who had been allowed in during the summer months, due to structural concerns. A detailed inspection, commissioned by Scarborough Borough Council, revealed structural faults to the central column which supports the spiral staircase running through the centre of the lighthouse. It has been estimated that £200,000 will be needed to repair the two stone lighthouses, and even more expensive repairs may be needed for the piers themselves.

The four Whitby harbour lights illuminated after dusk.
ROBIN JONES

CHAPTER 23

WHITBY HIGH

UNLIKE THE HARBOUR lights, Whitby's Trinity House lighthouse is not visible from the town, and stands on Ling Hill, near High Hawsker 2 miles along the Cleveland Way coastal footpath to the south east.

It is referred to as Whitby High to distinguish it from those guarding the entrance to the harbour.

The lighthouse is operated and maintained by Trinity House, which ordered it to be built in 1857.

What you see today was one of a pair of lighthouses built on the hill by Trinity House's chief engineer James Walker, who was also president of the Institution of Civil Engineers from 1834 to 1845.

The pair, High Light and South Light, were aligned in a north to south formation, showing fixed lights over Whitby Rock. The first light was shone in them on 1 October, 1858.

In 1890, a more efficient light was installed in High Light,

The almost precarious position of Trinity House's Whitby High lighthouse, pictured on a June dawn.
ROBIN JONES

making the lower one redundant, and it was closed down and demolished.

Of somewhat traditional lighthouse design, a white octagonal brick tower with lantern and gallery attached to a single-storey keeper's house, Whitby High is of a squat appearance, its tower being only 43ft high, compared to the 66ft of the South Light. However, because it is perched on 200ft cliffs, Whitby High has a focal plane of 240ft above mean high water.

White light has an intensity of 39,800 candela and the red light 17,100 candela.

The white light can be seen for 18 nautical miles and the red light for 16 nautical miles

Originally running on paraffin and electrified in 1976, the lighthouse was automated in 1992 and is today monitored and controlled via a telemetry link from the Trinity House Central Planning Unit at Harwich.

Its lantern houses three 250W 24V tungsten halogen lamps mounted on a LC45 two-position lamp changer. The optic is a six-panel 2nd order catadioptric drum.

James Walker, the Trinity House chief engineer who designed and built Whitby High and South lighthouses.

It emits a white or red light, depending on direction, five seconds on and five seconds off.

On the site of the demolished lighthouse, a single-storey foghorn station was built, with a giant horn on the roof nicknamed the Whitby or Hawsker Bull, and which first sounded, or rather bellowed, on 4 January, 1904. Before that, there had been a local campaign against the positioning of a foghorn because of public health fears over the noise.

The power supply for the horn was provided by two horizontal 25 horsepower oil engines, working at 210 revolutions per minute to compress the vast amount of air needed to sound the 20ft long and 8ft high horns. One of the horns faces north, and the other south-east.

It has been said that the sound travelled at such a low velocity that when a first blast was heard in Whitby, the third was being emitted at the foghorn station. Needless to say, operating staff were warned to use ear protectors.

The manager of the station lived in the main building and his deputy in adjoining accommodation.

The horn was replaced with an electronic hooter in 1988. The station was sold off as a smallholding with an acre of land, at one stage renamed Hornblower Lodge, but the horns are still very much in place on the roof.

An early Edwardian view of Whitby High lighthouse, possibly with the keeper's family. AUTHOR'S COLLECTION

The lighthouse complex viewed from behind.
IAN COWE/TRINITY HOUSE

Whitby High lighthouse and keepers' cottages today.
ROBIN JONES

CHAPTER 24
SCARBOROUGH

SCARBOROUGH'S HARBOUR lighthouse holds a unique place in this book, in that it is the only one destroyed as a result of enemy bombing.

In the same raid of 16 December, 1914 in which the Imperial German Navy bombarded Hartlepool and Whitby, Scarborough was first targeted.

At 8am, battlecruisers *Derfflinger* and *Von der Tann* began shelling the town with their 12, 11 and 5.9-in guns. Scarborough Castle, the Grand Hotel, three churches and more than 200 other properties were struck by a total of 520 shells, with 18 people killed, either instantly, or later dying as a result of their injuries.

People rushed to the railway station and the roads leading out of the town.

The lighthouse on Vincent or Vincent's Pier, now commonly referred to as Lighthouse Pier, was the last to be hit, with a shell tearing a gaping hole in the upper part of the tower as the Germans' parting shot. A shell also damaged the harbourmaster's living quarters. At 8.25am, the bombardment stopped and the

Scarborough lighthouse is today the centrepiece of the town harbour.
ROBIN JONES

battlecruisers moved north to nearby Whitby, where a coastguard station was shelled. Whitby Abbey and other buildings in the town were also hit, and seven people died.

The attack on the three towns caused a total of 137 fatalities and 592 casualties, many of whom were civilians. It created public outrage towards the German navy for an attack against civilians, and against the Royal Navy for its failure to prevent the raid.

The attack became part of a British propaganda campaign, 'Remember Scarborough', used on army recruitment posters. Editorials in neutral America condemned the attack and young men in their droves rushed to their local recruitment offices to avenge Scarborough, Whitby and Hartlepool.

Archaeologist Bob Clarke said that at the time Scarborough was described in maritime literature as a 'defended town' due primarily to the castle site. Furthermore, the town had three radio stations, with state-of-the-art technology for the Royal Navy. He said that the shell patterns suggested that these were the key targets for the raid, not the local inhabitants as was widely reported at the time.

Scarborough suffered heavily during the war, with up to 12 trawlers sunk in one night by German submarines. It has been said that enemy action led to the town's decline as a port.

The Germans returned to Scarborough in December 1917 when a U-boat surfaced 4 miles offshore and blasted the harbour with 30 rounds of shells, half of which fell on fishing and pleasure boats.

Another recorded hit by a German bomb on a UK land lighthouse was that at St Catherine's near Ventnor on the Isle of Wight, when on 1 June, 1943, a direct hit during a Luftwaffe raid destroyed the engine house killing the three keepers on duty who had taken shelter in the building.

The damaged top half of Scarborough's lighthouse was demolished three days after the direct hit, leaving only the lower part standing.

The Asquith government offered no money to rebuild it under war damage reparations, despite its importance to the fishermen and livelihood of the town. The lighthouse was insured

The gaping hole left in Scarborough's lighthouse after it was hit by the last of 520 shells fired on the top by German battlecruisers on 16 December, 1914. AUTHOR'S COLLECTION

A rainbow breaks over Scarborough's harbour and lighthouse.
DOM PATES*

only for its original £500 cost and repairs alone were double that. The Scarborough Townsmens Guild had to raise the £1,800 needed to repair the lighthouse and another £425 for the adjoining Pier House from public donations. It was to be fourteen years before the lighthouse shone a light again.

There was a Roman signal station at Scarborough, built around 370. However, the town was founded by two Icelandic Viking raiders, Thorgills Ogmundarson and his brother Kormak, who sometime after 966 founded the stronghold called Skarthaborg which took its name from a nickname of Thorgills, Skarthi, meaning hare-lip. As well as a raiding base, a fishing community sprang up.

Scarborough's harbour in South Bay at the foot of

Scarborough Castle Hill has three piers, the earliest, the West Pier, built after 1325, the East Pier after 1811 and the Vincent Pier in 1752. The latter pair were built under the provisions of an act of Parliament of 1732, William Vincent constructing the one named after him.

The three piers enclose the outer and inner harbour. The outer harbour is used mainly by pleasure craft. The inner harbour is used by fishing and passenger boats. The outer harbour is tidal and almost dries out at low water.

The earliest record of a lighthouse on Vincent Pier was in 1804, and it may have been built up to three years earlier. Another reference, in 1806, mentions a brick-built flat-topped circular building surrounded by railings with a coal brazier on its

Rough seas break over Vincent Pier, as depicted in a late Victorian illustration. AUTHOR'S COLLECTION

A pleasure steamer berths alongside Vincent Pier, in an Edwardian hand-coloured postcard view showing the lighthouse in its pre-1914 form. AUTHOR'S COLLECTION

roof designed by a surveyor called Nixon. It is unclear as to whether this structure was the same building mentioned earlier.

To show when there was at least 12ft of water in the harbour, a red flag was displayed during the day and the light at night. Such a light would have been unreliable due to the wind and height of the waves.

The brazier was superseded by a light comprising six tallow candles, the intensity of which was after a few years enhanced by a tin and in 1818 a copper reflector. A night watchman was employed to ensure that the candles stayed burning.

An extension to the building was added in 1843 as accommodation for the keeper and harbourmaster, and the following year, the tower was increased in height by 17ft, with a lantern room and gallery added. The candles were also replaced by gas lights, causing a local protest because their whitish colour was markedly different from the reddish tinge given out by the candles. Ship owners complained that they could not make out the light against the backdrop of white lights on the shore and nearby areas.

The issue was settled when Trinity House recognised and approved the decision of the local Harbour Authority.

The gas-fuelled lantern, called the Bude light, emitted a brilliant and powerful beam, but fuel bills soared. In 1845, it was replaced by a smaller 4in burner, comprising five gaslights, two of which were lit permanently during long winter nights. The white was visible for 4 miles.

A tidal gauge was installed at the head of the pier and a black ball superseded the flag that had been used for daylight warnings.

In 1847 a portable lamp was provided for use in emergencies such as gas failure.

Three years later, an additional storey was added to the adjoining main building.

The lighthouse had been electrified by World War One.

The rebuilt lighthouse was officially reopened on 22 December, 1931. At first it displayed a red light, which again caused anger and confusion: this time, townsfolk complainted that there were too many red lights on the shore. Trinity House again intervened, and the light was changed to a white isophase version.

The 'new' lighthouse comprised a 49ft white conical brick tower with an octagonal domed lantern room.

The rebuilt lighthouse had a foghorn which was used as an air raid siren during World War Two.

In 1940, Scarborough Borough Council took over the running of the port from the Harbour Commissioners. The keeper's house, last used by the harbourmaster and his family in 1937, has been used as an office and clubhouse by Scarborough Yacht Club since 1952.

A new lantern room was installed during the 1980s, but the remainder of the tower is as rebuilt in 1931.

The light has a focal plane of 56ft and its main white isophase light is displayed 2.5 seconds on and 2.5 seconds off. There is also a pair of fixed green lights looking out to sea. A foghorn sounds a blast every sixty seconds.

The lighthouse is supplemented by navigation aids elsewhere in the harbour. Two vertical fixed red lights which can be seen 4 miles out to sea are mounted on top of a watch hut on West Pier, and a flashing green East Pier, visible for 3 miles, is fixed to the top of a 13ft steel mast.

The lighthouse is currently operational, but manned only during the summer months, since the last twenty-four-hour watch was carried out in 1997. By then, the number of boats using the port had fallen sharply, due to European quotas and catch restrictions making it more difficult for local fishermen to earn a living.

The harbourmaster is now personally responsible for the permanent supervision of the lighthouse. Workers at the lighthouse are known as tidal officers: their role includes checking the boats are berthed safely and operating the foghorn and pier bridge. Storm shutters over the rear windows are still closed manually during bad weather.

Since the 1870s, there have been tales of hauntings in the lighthouse. The ghost of harbourmaster Captain Appleyard who drowned after falling into the harbour has been seen on several occasions. Witnesses said he had been seen sitting in his office, and walking through a wall and even smelling his pipe smoke. One worker was said to have been so scared by the apparition that he refused to set foot on the pier again.

Now run by Scarborough Ports and owned and managed by the borough council, the lighthouse is open to the public every day in summer, including evening visits.

Scarborough lighthouse is now fronted by the Diving Belle, commissioned from artist Craig Knowles by Scarborough Civic Trust and unveiled in May 2007. It represents the Scarborough of the present. ALLAN HARRIS*

CHAPTER 25

FLAMBOROUGH HEAD

FLAMBOROUGH HEAD lies at the tip of an 8-mile promontory between Filey and Bridlington bays which comprises Britain's only northern chalk sea cliffs.

The name Flamborough, spelled in the Domesday Book as Flaneberg, is possibly from the Saxon word "flaen" meaning a dart, which the shape of the headland resembles. It is also home to what is recognised as the country's oldest complete lighthouse.

In 1669, Middlesex speculator Sir John Clayton together with a George Blake petitioned Charles II for permission to build lighthouses at five locations on the east coast, including one at Flamborough Head and others on the Farne Islands and at Spurn Head.

Trinity House in London voiced its opposition so that it could safeguard its ancient rights of controlling navigational aids. Despite the king signing letters patent for the lighthouses on 25 October that year, a legal battle against Clayton and Blake ensued.

At Flamborough Head in 1674, Clayton erected a 79ft four-stage octagonal white tower built from coursed chalk rubble with stone dressings and a brick parapet, with rectangular windows to the upper three stages on the seaward side. The light was to have been provided by a brazier at the top burning coal or brushwood.

However, it is widely believed that no light was ever shone from it, as was the case with another of his lighthouses, at Foulness Point near Cromer.

Flamborough Head lighthouse and foghorn station as seen from the air.
PETER LAMB/TRINITY HOUSE

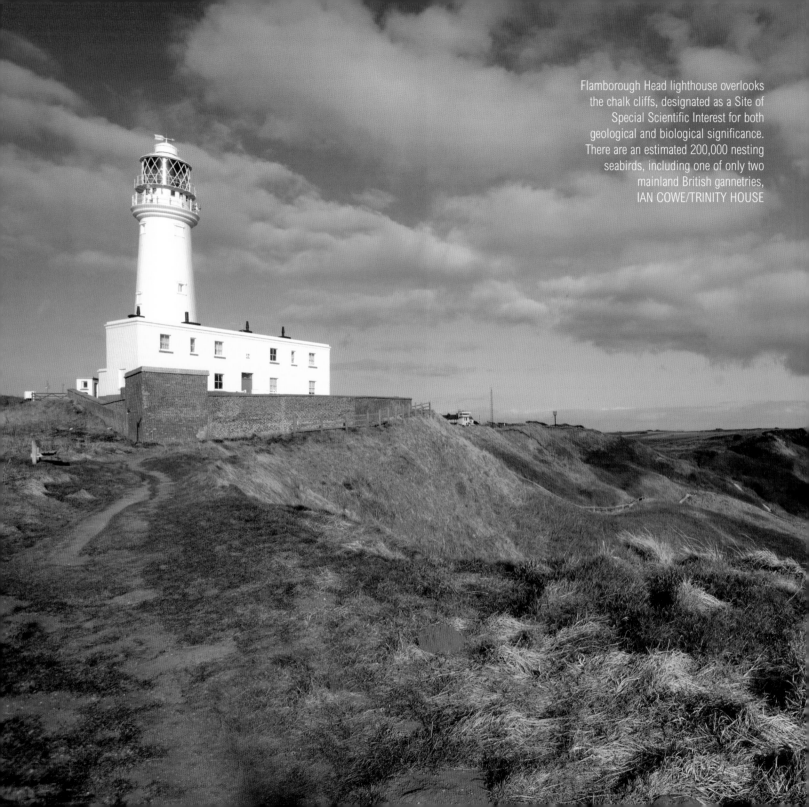

Flamborough Head lighthouse overlooks the chalk cliffs, designated as a Site of Special Scientific Interest for both geological and biological significance. There are an estimated 200,000 nesting seabirds, including one of only two mainland British gannetries, IAN COWE/TRINITY HOUSE

The spiral staircase inside Flamborough Head lighthouse is shaped almost like one of the ammonites that you would find in the chalk cliffs. ANDREW STAWARZ*

Further protests from Trinity House led to Charles II bowing to pressure and referring the dispute to the Committee for Trade and Plantations for an inquiry. At the same time, Trinity House campaigned for shipmasters not to pay any fees to him for his lights.

The location of the tower at Flamborough Head suggests that sailors would have found it difficult to see its coal-powered light in poor visibility.

Because of the legal objections, Clayton eventually surrendered the patent for his lighthouses apart from the one at Corton, between Great Yarmouth and Lowestoft, the only one to be lit. He ended up bankrupt.

While his other lighthouses have long since disappeared, the one at Flamborough Head, now in the care of East Riding of Yorkshire Council, and standing in Lighthouse Road near the fifth tee of Flamborough Head Golf Club is in a remarkable state of preservation, and is Grade II* listed. In 1996, it was restored, with 20 tons of chalk replacing the severely-corroded north face and all the floors and roof renewed, the £100,000 cost being met by English Heritage and East Yorkshire Borough Council.

What seems amazing was that it took so long to build a lighthouse at Flamborough, at the tip of a jagged dangerous coast long feared by sailors, because of its numerous chalk reefs and outcrops hidden by the waves and the strong currents funnelled past the head. Such a light would benefit not only coasters but deep sea vessels from the Baltic plying their trade to England.

The earliest recorded shipwreck off Flamborough Head was in 1348 when the sailing boat *La Katerine* became stranded on the rocks during a raging storm. Around 175 vessels were wrecked there between 1770 and 1806, averaging one every twelve weeks.

By 1806, Trinity House had become convinced that a lighthouse at Flamborough would save lives.

Designed by Samuel Wyatt, and set much closer to the water than Clayton's, Bridlington builder John Matson was commissioned to build it, along with the adjoining keepers' cottages. Remarkably, he used no scaffolding and completed the tower in nine months. It first shone on 1 December that year.

Above left: Sir John Clayton's Flamborough Head octagonal chalk lighthouse tower was built in 1669 with the permission of Charles II, but was probably never used. ROBIN JONES

Above right: The Trinity House lighthouse at Flamborough Head was built in 1806. ROBIN JONES

The original lighting apparatus was designed by George Robinson and consisted of a rotating vertical shaft with 21 parabolic reflectors fixed to it, seven on each of the three sides of the frame. The light was provided by an oil lamp driven by a clockwork motor. It had a candle power of 13,860.

To distinguish it from the lighthouse at Cromer, red glass-covered reflectors were installed on each side, providing for the first time anywhere, two white flashes followed by one red flash. This innovation was eagerly taken up by lighthouse designers elsewhere.

In 1925, the tower was raised to its present 87ft height, with a focal plane of 213ft.

The lighthouse was electrified in 1940, and further modifications took place in 1974.

An electric fog signal was installed in 1975 replacing the diaphone apparatus powered by compressed air. In previous times, a rocket was discharged from the headland every five minutes in foggy weather, reaching an altitude of 600ft. In 1992 a 1000-watt halogen bulb was installed. The lighthouse became automatic in 1996, with the lamp changer and optic drive replaced by standard Trinity House equipment, and the last keepers leaving on 8 May. The fog signal was refurbished and a standard fog detector fitted. It sounds two blasts every ninety seconds.

The lighthouse is now controlled and monitored from Harwich. It was repainted in 2010.

The light, which uses a 1st Order catadioptric rotating optic, emits four white flashes every fifteen seconds, and can be seen for nearly 28 miles. Its peak intensity is 650,000 candela.

While it is not possible to access Clayton's tower, the Trinity House lighthouse has a visitor centre, open on certain days of the season.

Flamborough lighthouse with the winter constellation of Orion as a background. PAUL WILLOWS*

CHAPTER 26
BRIDLINGTON

FAMOUS FOR ITS shellfish, Bridlington is a fishing port and working harbour, through which the Gypsey Race river enters the sea.

It was inhabited as long ago as the Bronze Age and it is believed that the port existed before the Roman conquest. It is speculated that Gabrantovicorum Roman maritime station, was located where the present-day town now stands.

A fourth-century series of signal stations designed to warn of attacks by Saxon raiders was likely to have included Bridlington, where a central fort was sited, some historians conjecture.

The sheltered spot below the promontory of Flamborough Head became known as Bridlington Bay, and the area occupied by the present-day port was originally called Bridlington Quay.

A chalybeate spring was discovered there in 1805, during the heyday of Britain's spa towns, the forerunners of seaside resorts. The port's first hotel was opened that year and Bridlington took off as a resort popular with industrial workers from West Riding, especially after the coming of the railway in October 1846.

Bridlington Bay has for centuries been viewed as a fairly safe place for sheltering ships in high winds.

To replace earlier wooden piers that were susceptible to storm damage, the North Pier was, according to English Heritage, constructed from large ashlar stone blocks between 1816-37, and extended in 1868.

A lighthouse station was established on the pier in 1852, when a 28ft white lamp-post-style light was erected at the north end. The cast-iron lamp-post has a square battered base, fluted shaft and an octagonal lantern.

Operated by Bridlington Harbour Authority, the post light

The Victorian cast-iron post light at the end of Bridlington's North Pier is still giving sterling service. ROBIN JONES

The disused cast-iron post light
on the northern harbour wall.
DAVID PICKERSGILL*

This lighthouse motif is laid out on a grassy slope overlooking Bridlington harbour. ROBIN JONES

has a focal plane of 39ft and emits a white flash every two seconds, which is visible for 5 miles.

Red and green harbour control lights and a yellow fog signal which sounds once a minute are mounted on the side of the post. The green light is shown when there is less than 9ft of water in the harbour entrance, and the red light when there is more than 9ft.

A similar light lamp which stands on the northern edge of the harbour is disused. During daylight, a red flag flying near the end of the later South Pier indicates a depth of more than 9ft in the entrance.

East Riding Council, the harbour authority and regeneration company Yorkshire Forward have for several years been working on a scheme for a new 320-berth marina alongside a revamped fishing harbour. If the plans go ahead, a new navigational light is likely to have to be provided.

Both the North and later South Piers enjoy Grade II listed building protection.

CHAPTER 27
WITHERNSEA

IN RESPONSE TO the high number of shipwrecks occurring at Withernsea because vessels could not see the lights at either Flamborough Head or Spurn, Trinity House eventually responded to public pressure and ordered a lighthouse to be built there.

Before the seaside resort's pier was swept away in a storm in 1880, there had been instances of it being damaged by ships colliding with it in the night.

Originally 399 yards long, the pier became shorter and shorter with each major crash. The *Saffron* struck the pier in 1880, and there were further crashes in 1888 and 1893, which reduced it to just 50ft. The pier was removed in 1903, but the sandstone towers which form the entrance remain as one of the town's landmarks.

The 12ft white-painted octagonal brick and concrete lighthouse tower was designed either by Sir James Douglass or Thomas Matthews for Trinity House and built between 1892-94 by Strattens of Edinburgh, intended to help guide ships into the Humber estuary with the aid of other lights to the south.

The lighthouse was built as close to the coast as deemed practical. Back then, a huge expanse of sand dunes divided it from the beach, but it was decided not to build it any closer to the water because of the notorious coastal erosion. However, with the building of a promenade across the sea front, and backfilling behind it by houses as Withernsea grew as a resort, the tower in Hull Road ended up in the middle of the town, nearly a quarter of a mile from the sea, and is often described as an inland lighthouse.

A spiral staircase of 144 steps leads to the lantern gallery and service room at the top. There are no dividing floors to provide

One of the last Withernsea lighthouse keepers with the light which Trinity House took to its visitor centre at St Mary's Island lighthouse in Whitley Bay. WITHERNSEA LIGHTHOUSE MUSEUM

accommodation for the keepers, who lived in two adjoining cottages,

Originally the light was powered by an eight-wick paraffin lamp in an octaganal revolving lens.

The lens weighed two tons and floated in a bath of three gallons of mercury.

The mechanism that turned the lens was wound daily by hand.

The light was converted to electricity in 1936, although the paraffin lamp was kept as a standby. A 100 volt 1500 watt bulb with an intensity of 800,000 candela produced a light visible for 17 miles.

The lighthouse was declared redundant in 1976 and the light was turned off from 1 July that year. The lens was reused by St Mary's lighthouse in Whitley Bay, replacing one which ended up at the former lighthouse museum in Penzance.

In October 1985, the lighthouse and adjoining keepers' houses became a Grade II listed building.

The following year, the lighthouse was sold by Trinity House to the Campbell family, relatives of Kay Kendall, the 1950s film star who was born Justine Kay MacCarthy at Stanley House a few doors further up Hull Road.

The family intended to turn it into a memorial to the star of much-loved films like the car classic comedy *Genevieve*, who made

Kay Kendall, who appeared in films alongside Hollywood stars like Gene Kelly and Yul Brynner. WITHERNSEA LIGHTHOUSE MUSEUM

Withernsea lighthouse today towers over the middle of the resort.
ROBIN JONES

Before the days of the motor car: an Edwardian postcard view of Hull Road and Withernsea's inland lighthouse.
AUTHOR'S COLLECTION

The 127ft Withernsea lighthouse dominates the flat landscape of the town.
ROBIN JONES

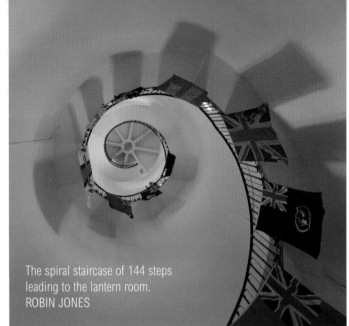

The spiral staircase of 144 steps leading to the lantern room.
ROBIN JONES

View from the top: the lantern room offers a sweeping panorama of the town below. HJSP2*

A rear view of the lighthouse from the back garden, with the keepers' cottages in front now housing a café and museum rooms. ROBIN JONES

her film debut at the age of nineteen and who died from leukaemia in 1959 at the age of thirty-three.

It was taken over by the Withernsea Lighthouse Museum Trust, a registered charity, in 1989, and was converted into an excellent museum, with one of the rooms dedicated to Kay Kendall memorabilia, with pictures and short clips from her films.

Other ground floor displays include a local history room with a scale model of Withernsea railway station, a victim of the Beeching Axe, and a history of the lifeboats at Withernsea and Spurn and local coastguards. There is a museum café in one of the keeper's houses with tables in the rear garden.

There is no longer any light apparatus in the gallery, from which visitors can enjoy spectacular views across the town and Holderness. There is, however, a webcam, which operates between 7am and 8pm every day and pans across Withernsea during opening hours.

The lighthouse and its museum is not run to make a profit. All money raised is ploughed back into developing the exhibits.

It is open on Saturday and Sunday afternoon between Easter and October, and weekdays from June until mid September.

The exhibition about local lifeboats and the coastguard service at the bottom of the lighthouse tower. ROBIN JONES

CHAPTER 28
SPURN HEAD

"Behind Hull is the plain of Holderness, lonelier and lonelier, and after that the birds and lights of Spurn Head, and then the sea."

Philip Larkin

SPURN HEAD IS the classic example of a sandspit so beloved by geography teachers. Formed at the mouth of the Humber, it comprises sand, shingle and boulder clay washed down from the notoriously erosion-prone Holderness coast from Flamborough Head southwards by a process of longshore drift, and is the fastest eroding coastline in Europe.

On the eastern side of the sandspit is the sea, and on the other side the river, or at low tide, huge expanses of mudflats. It is as little as 50 yards wide in places, and more than 3 miles long. Furthermore, it is constantly moving, altering its shape as more debris is washed down the coast to replace that which is lost in sea storms and surges. The spit is believed to be moving westwards by around 7ft each year. It has been said that a cycle of complete destruction of the spit and reconstruction occurs around every 250 years.

In the Middle Ages, Spurn Head was home to the port of Ravenspurn where the exiled Henry Bolingbroke landed in 1399 on his return to England before usurping Richard II to become Henry IV. Ravenspurn and another village, Ravenser Odd were lost to the sea as Spurn Head moved westwards.

Strong tidal currents and shifting sandbanks had for centuries presented a major problem for sailors accessing the Humber, and

The Low Light surmounted by a water tank stands in the water, while the High Light dominates the grassy 'hillock' in the centre of Spurn Head.
HUMBER ESTUARY SERVICES

An aerial view of Spurn Head from the south, showing the Low Light of 1852 to the left, and the High Light centre. HUMBER ESTUARY SERVICES

conjectured that it comprised a stone tower with a brazier to burn coal or wood on top, but we did not know what happened to it.

Hull Trinity House, which was believed to have placed a number of sea marks in the estuary, proposed in 1590 that a lighthouse should be built on Spurn Head. The increase in coastal trade, particularly the carrying of coal from Tyneside to London, stepped up the pressure for more effective navigational aids, but nothing came of the proposal.

Many more proposals followed in the decades to come, but so often they met with hostility from the Brethren of the Trinity Houses, who regarded lighthouses with suspicion.

Bids or requests to build lighthouses at Spurn came in 1618 by Peter Frobisher, heir and executor of explorer Sir Martin Frobisher, the widow of Sir James Ouchterlony, a Gentleman of the Privy Chamber to James I, in 1634, Thomas Stratton of Boston 1657, shipmasters trading to Newcastle and beyond in 1660, Royalist Colonel Philip Frowde the following year and Charles Whittington, Searcher of the Customs at Hull, in 1671.

In 1672, Justinian Angell, grandson of William Angell who had been granted Spurn by James I in 1609, launched his own scheme. He claimed he had been approached, as the local landowner, by coastal traders, who wanted to end a stalemate between Frowde and Hull Trinity House over the issue.

After Angell offered £50 a year to the poor fund of Hull Trinity House, four Elder Brethren visited the site and declared it was to view the proposed site and they reported it was 'the fittingest place' for a lighthouse.

The following year, Trinity House in London objected to Angell's plan, because ships from London, Ipswich or Yarmouth bound for Newcastle who would pay dues would miss the estuary mouth completely, picking up the coast again beyond Flamborough Head, and also feared that the proposed light would be on low land and could not be seen by ships until several other dangers had passed.

Accordingly, royal assent was refused, but Angell broke all the rules and started building a pair of lighthouses, fearing that Clayton, who was busy building his tower at Flamborough Head,

if a lighthouse was to be built, Spurn Head would be an obvious choice as it stretched around a third of the way across the estuary mouth.

The first reference to a lighthouse on the sandspit was on 28 November, 1427 when William Reedbarrow, a hermit, was granted permission from Edward VI to extract dues from passing ships to finance one he was building there. It was a charitable as opposed to profitable venture, but no other details survive. It is

An 1820s' ink etching of Smeaton's High Light of 1746 and the Low Light, one of many that were washed away. TRINITY HOUSE

The Spurn Head lighthouses and surrounding small community at the beginning of the 20th century. AUTHOR'S COLLECTION

might get in first.

Angell arranged with one Catlyn, a Hull master builder, to meet him at King's Lynn to view some lighthouses and work out how to build a pair at Spurn Head.

The determined Angell then chose a site on the sandspit by lighting fires around it and then sailing out to sea and seeing which shone the brightest.

Angell's High Light was said to be a 60ft octagonal brick tower, possibly similar to Clayton's Flamborough Head tower, with a coal fire hanging in an iron basket on top. The basket was capable of being raised another 14 feet if necessary. This first Low Light was a temporary affair.

In the meantime, tidal currents created a new dangerous sandbank at the mouth of the Humber, with fresh demands for new navigational marks being made.

On 10 April, 1675, Angell lit his lights for the first time. The furious Brethren of Hull Trinity House, who had wanted to see lights built instead at nearby Dimlington, where they owned land, obtained an order demanding that he extinguish them, which was done by the keeper when the notice was served on him on 14 May.

Angell, meanwhile, who was also opposed by the diarist Samuel Pepys, warden of the London Trinity House, was busy mustering up support. Nature came to his aid when a buoy that had been placed on the new sand drifted away again, and in October that year, Charles II granted him a patent for the lighthouses.

He then improved the low light, which may have been a smaller version of the high light, but nobody today is sure.

The affair nearly bankrupted Angell in legal costs and other expenses, not least of all having to pay for high quality coal for the lights to be shipped in from Newcastle and carried over the sand and shingle.

On 26 November, 1703, on the far side of England, a great storm washed away the first Eddystone lighthouse with its builder, Henry Winstanley, inside it. The same storm also shook the Spurrn high light, the wind causing the fire to burn so strongly that the brazier bars melted.

In December 1715, the westward movement on the spit saw the low light succumb to the sea, but seeing the urgency of replacing it, Hull Trinity House helped Angell's son John to do so. The low light was washed away again on 25 January, 1752,

Looking north from the gallery of Spurn Head lighthouse.
HARRY WATKINS

and was subsequently rebuilt only 70ft from the high light, rendering it of modest usefulness. The sea took it again on 14 February, 1763, and yet again on 4 December. It was clear that new lights were needed. But much legal wrangling took place before an Act of Parliament was passed on 14 May, 1766, empowering the removal of the existing lighthouses and replacing them.

It was in 1767 that John Smeaton, who built the successful third Eddystone lighthouse, as described in my book *Lighthouses of the South West*, was asked by both the London and Hull Trinity Houses to design and build two new lighthouses on Spurn Head.

The coal-burning lights in the pair of brick towers built 280 yards apart, were first lit on 5 September, 1776, replacing temporary lights. However, within two years, Smeaton's Low Light, a 50ft version of his 90ft High Light tower, was itself swept away, to be replaced for many years by a swape, a lever for hoisting a basket of burning coals mounted on a wooden frame, rather than a new tower.

A new Low Light tower complete with Argand lamp and reflectors was built by John Shaw in 1816 and first shone on 25 November that year, but it was abandoned in January 1830 after it was undermined by the sea and collapsed soon afterwards. The last Spurn lighthouse to be built for the Angell family, it was replaced by a wooden tower carrying a lantern.

Legislation empowered London Trinity House to buy the Spurn Head lights in 1840. The Low Light was destroyed in a storm surge in December 1851, but the lighting apparatus was salvaged and a new 50ft tower was built on the Humber foreshore the following year, coming into operation on 24 June.

The 1895 lighthouse and keepers' cottages as depicted on an Edwardian hand-coloured postcard view. AUTHOR'S COLLECTION

Right: An incandescent triple-mantle oil burner from Spurn Head lighthouse, a type developed by Sir Thomas Matthews, engineer-in-chief of London Trinity House. The oil is vaporised by the hot gases rising from the mantles, the coil being shielded by asbestos at the top. ROBIN JONES

In 1883, the Spurn light was made an occulting rather than fixed light, with a three-second dark interval in every thirty seconds.

London Trinity House discovered in 1892 that cracks were appearing in Smeaton's High Light tower, and a new tower was needed.

The 128ft round brick tower with lantern and gallery and painted with black and white horizontal bands was designed by Sir Thomas Matthews, London Trinity House engineer-in-chief from 1982-1915. Lit by oil, its white light which flashed every twenty seconds could be seen for 17 miles.

As three subsidiary lights shone from several levels of the tower – a fixed white light at 60ft shining towards the Chequer Shoal, a fixed red light at 60ft towards the Haile Sand Buoy, both with a range of 13 miles, and a fixed white light at 45ft directed up the river – the low light became redundant.

While Smeaton's tower was dismantled after the new High Light shone for the first time in 1895 – its foundations next to the replacement structure can still be seen today – the black-painted Low Light was left in place but minus its lantern and gallery.

At one stage it became used as an explosives store, and later a 20,000 gallon water tank, for supplying the small community at Spurn, was installed on the top of the tower. It remains in that state to this day, although the tank has long been disused.

Spurn Head not only once had its own railway, but also passenger-carrying vehicles that were powered by sail.

The standard gauge railway ran for 3¾ of a mile from a northern terminus at Godwin Battery in Kilnsea to Green Battery at the tip of the head.

With the onset of World

War One and concerns over the threat of German forces to the ports of Hull, Grimsby, Immingham and Killingholme, then newly-established as an oil terminal, the War Department gave top priority to defending the Humber.

Two massive island forts were built in the estuary – Haile Sand Fort on the low water mark near Cleethorpes, and Bull Fort on a sandbank in the middle of the Humber. These are covered in my companion volume: *Lighthouses of the East Coast: East Anglia and Lincolnshire*.

Two coastal gun batteries were installed at both ends of Spurn Head. The War Department built the railway to bring both men and materials to the new Spurn Head fortress, removing the necessity of a 3-mile walk over sand dunes. A railway pier complete with steam crane was built near the tip of Spurn Head to unload materials brought in by sea.

While steam locomotives were used to build the line and, from the 1920s, petrol-engine railcars appeared, the most unusual form of traction to be seen on it was a pair of sail bogies or trolleys, which appeared around 1915.

Wooden platforms with flanged wheels and a sail mast fixed in the centre, they were built and used by the lifeboatmen and the men working for the War Department, who often gave trips on them to visitors. They were also used by lighthouse staff.

Sail power was last used on the railway during or just after World War Two, when steam locomotion returned. A concrete road to Spurn Head was built, and the high light was electrified in 1941 to make the light easily available on request to allied shipping and convoys. The War Department installed a diesel-

The classic tower of the 1895 Spurn Head lighthouse. ANGELA FINDLAY*

The spiral staircase inside Spurn Head lighthouse. LEE BEAL/ YORKSHIRE WILDLIFE TRUST

driven plant on Spurn Head to supply both the lighthouse and the garrison.

The railway was closed in the winter of 1951-52 and dismantled, but sections of it can be seen embedded in the roadway. More about this line can be found in my book *Britain's Bizarre Railways*, also published by Halsgrove.

In the 1950s, Spurn Head was handed over to the care of the Yorkshire Wildlife Trust and it became a national nature reserve.

From 17 January, 1957, electricity was replaced by acetylene gas, and the subsidiary lights made occulting. The main light was changed to flash once every fifteen seconds. The pressure of the gas rotated the lantern and worked the occulting mechanism, making the keepers in the nearby cottages redundant. Although the mechanism was now automatic, Spurn Head lifeboatmen still had the responsibility of drawing the curtains in the lantern during the daytime, to prevent the lighting apparatus from catching fire. However, the keepers' houses and all the other buildings associated with the lighthouse were demolished.

Advances in navigation led to Trinity House declaring the lighthouse redundant, and it was switched off on 25 March, 1985, with the associated Spurn lightship, described in the next chapter, removed from its station on 11 December.

The Grade II listed lighthouse is now also owned by the trust. In September 2013, the Heritage Lottery Fund awarded £470,500 towards its restoration as a visitor centre with exhibitions and classrooms to open in 2015. Two former military buildings at the base of the lighthouse will be converted into a toilet block and a viewing platform.

The trust's chief executive Rob Stoneman said: "Spurn's lighthouse will once again become a beacon of light, celebrating the area's heritage and community spirit."

On 5 December, 2013, the sandspit was hit by a tidal surge which washed away much of the public road which runs along it after punching holes in the sea defences. The Environment Agency said the North Sea tidal surge was the worst since January 1953, when hundreds of people on the east coast of England as well as on the continent lost their lives.

Come the spring of 2014, with cars barred from accessing Spurn Head, visitors were left with a 3-mile walk from the trust's existing information centre on the north end of the spit, as landowners Associated British Ports discussed rebuilding the road. While natural processes are seeing the sandspit rebuild itself after the latest breach, the highest tides were still washing over parts of the curving peninsula.

A mosaic of Spurn Head lighthouse outside the Yorkshire Wildlife Trust's café near Kilnsea. ROBIN JONES

CHAPTER 29
SPURN AND OTHER HUMBER LIGHT VESSELS

THE HUMBER, the combined estuary of the Rivers Trent and Ouse, has been a major commercial seaway throughout history. The port of Kingston-upon-Hull, today commonly referred to as Hull, was built on seafaring, firstly whaling and later seafishing. While the fishing industry declined in the 1970s, the city remains a busy port, handling 13 million tonnes of cargo per year.

Long before the determined Justinian Angell built his lighthouses at Spurn Head, basic navigational marks such as buoys were placed at points in the estuary to warn ships about the dangers from shoals and sandbanks. However, with the increase in both shipping volumes and wrecks, it became clear that more needed to be done to mark out the entrance to the Humber.

What if a light could be placed on the water, rather than on land, giving round-the-clock warning of the dangers lurking beneath?

Although there are records of fire beacons being placed on Roman ships, the modern world's first lightship was placed at the Nore at the mouth of the River Thames by King's Lynn barber and ship manager Robert Hamblin and inventor David Avery in 1731. At first, London Trinity House regarded the lights as useless and raised objections, but soon saw its benefits and bought the patent itself. A second lightship was placed at the Dudgeon station off Norfolk five years later, and many more were to follow.

After buying the patent, all English and Welsh lightvessels were maintained by London Trinity House, with the exception of those maintained by the Mersey Docks and Harbour Board, and those in the Humber Estuary, which came under the Humber Conservancy Board.

A lightship station to aid with navigation into the Humber was established in 1820, warning of the notorious sandbanks

The Spurn lightship in 1902. HULL CITY COUNCIL

The current Spurn light float which occupies the position of the former Spurn lightship. HUMBER ESTUARY SERVICES

Humber Conservancy Board lightship No. 12 *Spurn* was built by Goole Shipbuilding and Repairing Company Ltd and spent forty-eight years guarding the entrance to the Humber estuary. She is now a floating museum in Hull Marina. ROBIN JONES

Top left: The lantern of No. 12 *Spurn*. ROBIN JONES

Top centre: The clockwork mechanism was responsible for rotating No. 12 *Spurn's* lantern. A falling weight regularly needed to be wound up to the top of the mast to keep the lantern turning. ROBIN JONES

Top right: This manual foghorn was carried on No. 12 *Spurn* in case the electric version lost power. Turning the handle produced a blast of compressed air that sent a penetrating sound through one of the trumpet-like poles on deck. ROBIN JONES

Bottom left: The binnacle on the Spurn lightship was a key part of its navigational system. Placed on the upper deck, it ensured that the ship had not drifted off position. While a metal ship causes problems for a magnetic compass, it has no effect on a binnacle which houses the compass and corrector magnets. ROBIN JONES

which lie south east of Spurn Head, where there had already been around 30 shipwrecks. From then on, a succession of manned vessels occupied the station, the best known of which is Humber Conservancy Board lightship No. 12 *Spurn*, if only because it is preserved in Hull Marina in Castle Street and open to the public on certain days free of charge.

This 100ft long Spurn lightship was built in 1927 by Goole Shipbuilding and Repairing Company Ltd for £17,000. Built of steel with seven watertight compartments, it was intended to be "practically unsinkable".

Not having an engine as is the case with many lightships, it was towed to Spurn lightship station in November that year.

The seven-man crew (in later years reduced to five) who were on board for a month at a time lived below deck, and took turns watching for passing ships. No. 12 has four sleeping berths, a washroom and a kitchen and galley stove. Food arrived every Wednesday in a supplies ship, and the crew were able to supplement it either by fishing or buying provisions from passing ships. Emergency rations were kept on board. In the early 1930s, a radio was fitted, and the ship was given the call sign MMH.

During World War Two, she was moved to the Middle Humber position, marking the boom across the river. The crew would sit in darkness, using torches to check the identity of approaching ships. It was permitted to display its much-reduced light only for Royal Navy and merchant navy vessels, and then only on days when the tides occurred during the hours of darkness. During the conflict, No. 12 was fired on by Luftwaffe machine gunners.

After 1945, she returned to Humber station, where she remained until 1959 when she was removed for refitting and painted red, her original colours having been black with white lettering. She was then transferred to Bull Shallows station, and became known as the 'Bull Light Vessel'. Decommissioned in 1975, she was eight years later acquired by Hull City Council which embarked on turning her into a floating museum, restoring her to her original condition and livery as the Spurn lightship.

No. 12 was towed to her present berth in the marina in October 1986 and opened to the public in February 2007.

When taken off station in 1959, she had been replaced by a newly-built lightship, Humber Conservancy Board No. 14.

This 114ft ship was built in 1959 at the Cook, Welton and Gemmell shipyard in Beverley for £98,843 and launched on 2 June that year, when it was blessed by a priest, reaching Spurn station on June 28.

Propulsion was provided by four Gardener diesel engines, and it had a crew of seven which was changed every fortnight. At first oil fired, the lamps were later changed to electric. Mounted on a rotating assembly, the light was focused via a Fresnel lens system. Although common in lighthouses, Fresnel lenses were rarely used on lightships. The ship also had a type of foghorn unique in British light vessels.

No. 14 was involved in several collisions on the station, firstly with the Hull trawler *Loch Seaforth* on 29 May, 1961, then with the Ostend trawler *Sea Lady* on 5 July that year, and finally with the Hull trawler *Steed Fame* on 17 October, 1966.

A mistake made by the crew on Christmas Eve 1982 led to the light not being displayed for five hours. On 19 December, 1984, it was visited by the Archbishop of York.

The Spurn station was decommissioned on December 11, 1985, bringing to an end nearly six centuries of manned lighthouses and lightships around Spurn Head.

In 1987, No. 14 was sold off privately and restored. In May 1988, she briefly became the headquarters of the Beaucette Yacht Club in Guernsey, renamed *Beaucette Lightship*.

Sold again that September, it was moved to Conwy in North Wales as a tourist attraction, and in October 1990 was bought for the Milford Haven Port Authority. It became a visitor attraction berthed in Milford Haven Marina, and the following year it was renamed *Haven* lightship.

No. 14 was sold to Irish tourism investors in July 1997, but by December 2001 it had laid up in Bantry Bay and was offered for sale.

On 1 June, 2007, she was bought by Dutch couple Jan and Agnes van der Elsen, who set out to turn it into an alternative healing centre under the banner of Lightship Therapies. They are

Light float *Humber*, in its previous livery of red and white stripes, in dry dock while being repainted by Coopers Painting Contractors Ltd of Grimsby. COOPERS PAINTING

Light float *Humber*, now painted green and back at Hull for maintenance, is normally stationed in the North Sea about 8 miles south east of Spurn Head. Owned and operated by Associated British Ports, it weighs about 70 tons, it is automatic and has a solar powered light and a racon, a radar transponder used to mark maritime navigational hazards. (RAdar and beaCON) fitted. There is also a small wind generator on board to keep the batteries topped up. HUMBER ESTUARY SERVICES

qualified practitioners offering therapies such as crystal healing, sound healing, reflexology, life-coaching, reiki, yoga, hot stone massages and aromatherapy.

In mid-November 2007, No. 14 was picked up by the tug *Sea Trojan* in Waterford and towed to the Sharpness Docks in Gloucester for restoration.

On 2 October, 2010, following three years of restoration and fitting out, the lightship, renamed *Sula* (meaning "little bit of peace"), was towed by a pair of tug boats up the Gloucester & Sharpness Ship Canal to its new permanent home at Llanthony Wharf in Gloucester Docks, where it also doubles up as the Gloucester Buddhist Centre and the owners' home.

Since the manned lightship was withdrawn, the Spurn station has been marked by the Spurn light float. A square skeletal tower enclosed by daymark panels and fixed to a catamaran hull, its lantern has a focal plane of 33ft and emits three quick white flashes every ten seconds as well as continuous white riding light. The float is painted black with a yellow horizontal band.

Another veteran Humber lightship is Trinity House LV91, which was built by Philip and Son Ltd of Dartmouth in 1937. Allocated to Humber station that year, it was damaged in a collision with the steamer *Maurice Rose* on 3 April, 1942, and again in a collision with the steamer *Armathia* on 1 September that year. From 1971-77, it was allocated to Helwick station off the Gower peninsula, hence the name in large letters on its hull. In 1977, she was acquired for preservation by the National Waterfront Museum at Swansea South Dock. She is on the Historic Ships Committee's Core Collection list because she still has many original fittings and is widely considered to be the best example of a preserved lightship in Britain today. ALEX LIIVET*

The Spurn lightship occupied one of five lightvessel stations on the Humber, the others being Bull, Lower Whitton, Middle Whitton and Upper Whitton.

The Middle Whitton lightship, which had a crew of three and marked sandbanks in the Upper Humber, was the furthest inland manned lightship in Britain.

Sailors and Whitton villagers once had a rhyme which warned of the dangers: *"Between Trent Falls and Whitton Ness, many are made widow and fatherless."*

In November 1875, Hull Trinity House informed the Board of Trade that it proposed to place a permanent floating lightship at Whitton Ness in place of a temporary vessel in use at the time. The new ship built by Richard Day of New Holland for £380 was installed on the station on 31 January, 1877.

In 1915, Joshua Watson of Gainsborough built *Audrey*, one of three vessels which served as the Middle, Upper and Lower Whitton lightship.

She was sold to the Sobriety project in Goole in 1986, and refurbished at a cost of £75,000, involving the conversion to the seagoing gaff-rigged ketch *Goole Billy Boy*. A version of a Humber keel or coastal sailing barge known as a Billy Boy, she is now used to give disadvantaged young people and community groups the experience of sailing at sea.

Further out to sea than the Spurn lightship station, lying around 8 miles south east of Spurn Head, can be found the

A 1:32 scale model of lightship *Bull*, built in 1909 by Earle's Shipbuilding and Engineering Co. Ltd of Hull for the Humber Conservancy Board, on display inside Hull Maritime Museum. Its station marked Bull Shallows where it was moored until 1959 when it was replaced by No. 12 *Spurn*. It had acetylene illumination with dioptric lenses and gave alternate red and white flashes, each of two thirds of a second duration, repeated every ten seconds. ROBIN JONES

Humber Conservancy Board lightship No. 14 took over Spurn station from No. 12 in 1959. When it was decommissioned in 1985, it was the last manned lightship in the Humber area. After passing through several owners it is now based at Gloucester Docks and renamed JAYT74.*

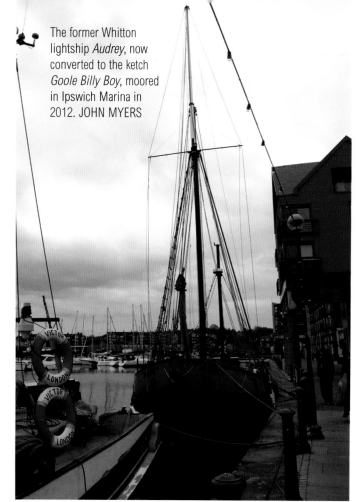

The former Whitton lightship *Audrey*, now converted to the ketch *Goole Billy Boy*, moored in Ipswich Marina in 2012. JOHN MYERS

modern lightfloat *Humber*. This unmanned 49ft vessel, for so long painted in red and white stripes but now pale green, also has its lantern carried on a square skeletal tower. With a focal plane of 33ft, it emits one long white flash every ten seconds.

Most British lightships were decommissioned during the 1970s and 1980s and replaced with similar light floats or LANBY (Large Automatic Navigation BuoY) buoys, the running costs of which are 10% of those of lightships. These navigation buoys are monitored remotely from onshore and run for extended periods without repair. The remaining UK lightships are now automated and unmanned and most use solar power.

To give an accurate description of every light float, buoy or other navigational aid in the Humber would be an encyclopaedic task and might well fill another book again. Today, the local lighthouse authority is ABP (Associated British Ports) Humber Estuary Services, in effect the successor to the Humber Conservancy Board. Its harbourmaster has responsibility for 113 floating navigational marks, 84 being buoys and the rest floats.

A further 29 shore marks are maintained and monitored by ABP, while the Port of Goole looks after 35 shore marks of its own.

ABP's list of all marks is updated regularly – it has to be, because the shifting sandbanks and current mean that there can be as many as 90 movements of seamarks in a year.

The Humber today is among the busiest and fastest-growing trading areas in Europe. Nearly a quarter of the UK's seaborne trade passes along the estuary, including 25% of the country's natural gas and 25% of its refined petroleum products. Despite the advances made in high-tech navigational aids which have seen so many lighthouses switched off, traditional seamarks will I suspect be around in the Humber for a very long time yet.

Thorngumbald Clough
High Light today.
ROBIN JONES

CHAPTER 30

THORNGUMBALD CLOUGH

THE PAIR OF wrought iron cylindrical lighthouses on the north bank of the Humber at Thorngumbald Clough date from 1870, and were built by the Brethren of Trinity House, Kingston upon Hull in response to changes in the deepwater river channel. Shifting sandbanks made the stone tower lighthouse at Paull described in the next chapter obsolete.

In 1868, the Brethren of Trinity House, Kingston upon Hull set up temporary marks on a trial basis that year, in a bid to ascertain the optimum position for new lights.

In February 1869, after the tests proved successful, the Brethren asked Trinity House in London for permission to erect four permanent lighthouses, two at Thorngumbald and another pair at Salt End, to indicate the middle of the deepwater channel from the No. 13 Hebbles Buoy to Victoria Dock. The request was granted, and all four were built by Thompson and Stather of Hull for a total of £1,064.

The pair at Thorngumbald Clough were erected on half an acre of land on the foreshore and were first shone in July 1870. There had been objections from the officer in charge of the army battery at Paull, part of the Humber sea defences, that they would block his line of fire in defence of the river. However, he dropped his objection when it was shown that they could be dismantled if war broke out. The High Light is a 49ft red cylindrical tower built out of riveted wrought iron girders fixed to brick and flagstone foundations, and with a focal plane of 50ft above high water. Its design was open lattice for two thirds of its height from the base with the top third covered in to protect the lantern and storeroom. A spiral staircase inside the open lattice

The Low Light, with the
High Light in the distance.
ROBIN JONES

The Thorngumbald Clough
lighthouses with the
keeper's cottage, now
demolished.

girders led to the storeroom from where the lantern was accessed by a ladder.

Its light was a holophote prismatic lens assisted by a prismatic reflector. The white fixed light could be seen 12½ miles away.

The Low Light, a 32ft white wrought iron cylindrical tower built 370ft in front of the High Light, was originally built on a rail-mounted trolley so that it could be moved if the sandbanks and deepwater channel shifted. With a focal plane of 28ft above high water, its fixed white light, originally powered by two oil burners, could be seen 10½ miles away.

Its railway track was extended by 15ft in 1888, when the light was moved 7ft 3in to align it correctly with the High Light.

The keeper's cottage for the pair was built close to the Low Light and was painted red.

The lights were also controlled by a clockwork switch and came on fifteen minutes prior to sunset and fifteen minutes after sunrise. Once a month the attendant would visit the lighthouses to wind up the mechanisms, which took into account the daily variation between sundown and sunrise.

The railway track was long since declared redundant, with the Low Light now fixed permanently to its base. The spiral staircase inside the lattice work of the High Light was replaced by a set of iron ladders. The keeper's cottage was demolished in 1998.

In 2003, implementing a policy of "managed retreat", a concept which found national favour from the 1990s onwards, the sea wall at this point was deliberately breached in a bid to return 80 hectares of the reclaimed flatland behind it to wetland. The basic concept is that rather than spending a fortune building and maintaining more coastal defences in the face of rising sea levels, let nature take its course. Wetland and mudflats act as a natural barrier in themselves, and absorb the force of incoming tides, while leaving a natural habitat for wildlife, in this case wildfowl and wading birds. Sounds good, but managed retreat came under scrutiny and criticism in early 2014 following the devastating flooding of the Somerset Levels, but that is another story.

At Thorngumbald Clough, moving both lights was considered, but it was finally decided to leave them in situ, on what

Against the background of the Humber Bridge floats No. 16 Sand End buoy, one of many floating navigational aids marking the deepwater channel to Hull, as seen from Thorngumbald Clough Low Light. ROBIN JONES

became a stone-reinforced peninsula between the wetland lagoon and the Humber. It is still possible to walk to them along the coast.

The fully operational lights are now under Associated British Ports, Hull jurisdiction. Both have been given Grade II listed building protection status by English Heritage.

Where there was dry land at Thorngumbald Clough in the 20th century, 80 hectares have been deliberately flooded to create a tidal wetland lagoon as part of a managed retreat policy. The High and Low lighthouses still stand in their historic positions on the horizon. ROBIN JONES

CHAPTER 31
PAULL

LYING 7 MILES to the east of Hull on the north bank of the Humber, the village of Paull has a distinctive lighthouse which has not been used for nearly a century and a half.

Ship owners had been constantly asking for a navigational aid on the approach to Hull where shifting sandbanks can change the course of the deepwater channel leading into the port. A basic beacon was said to have burned near the village, with a population today of just over 700, and the only riverside village east of Hull, since the 1770s.

Eventually, making a minimalist gesture, the Brethren of Trinity House of Kingston upon Hull paid seven shillings and sixpence for a house in Paull to be whitewashed so it could be used as a daymark.

Mariners demanded that more be done, and in 1835, the owner of the oldest inn in the village, the Humber Tavern, was paid £2 a month rent for a room from which a light could be shone over the estuary.

The following year, Hull's Trinity House ordered a proper lighthouse to be built on the shore. Architect Francis Dale was commissioned to design it, and came up with a circular brick tower with a lantern room on top, capped by a metal domed roof. Coated in cement, the 46ft lighthouse which was built as a separate, free-standing tower was originally painted red but later changed to its present white.

A lighthouse keeper, James Campbell, was appointed, and paid £50 a year. He lived in a two-storey cottage and attended the fixed white light.

In 1851, the light was improved when Thomas Purdon installed a red sector in addition to the white light, by placing a red glass in front of one of the reflectors. The light was shone

Paull lighthouse today, the cottages adjoining it having been built after it was erected. ANDY SIMPSON

The original Trinity House of Kingston upon Hull plaque on the front of Paull lighthouse. ROBIN JONES

THIS LIGHTHOUSE WAS BUILT 1836 BY THE TRINITY HOUSE OF KINGSTON UPON HULL WILLIAM COLLINSON GEORGE HALL. } WARDEN

from a rape seed oil-burning catoptric lantern of three lamps, and could be seen for 7 miles. A gas burner was later installed.

The windows of the lantern room face towards Hull. The light led ships to the safe channel when leaving the port. As ships left Hull, they would steer toward the light at Paull. From there, they would follow an alignment towards the Killingholme lighthouses on the south bank of the Humber and follow the channel further out into the estuary and into the North Sea.

After the sandbanks moved and caused the channel to shift, the Brethren looked at building a second light at Paull, but ditched the plans in favour of new ones at Thorngumbald Clough to the east and Salt End to the west. Paull's lighthouse accordingly became redundant in 1870.

For centuries, Paull had been the site of coastal defence batteries as it commanded a strategic position overlooking the river. After it was made redundant, the lighthouse was offered to the War Department for £450, but it declined to buy the property.

A terrace of coastguard cottages on the shore and another row on the street behind were later joined to the lighthouse tower by the infilling of the space between them by more cottages.

The row adjoining the lighthouse on the sea front is named Anson Villas after the wooden battleship HMS *Anson* which was launched in May 1812.

The building was transferred to the Humber Conservancy in 1908, but sold off privately in 1947, after it had fallen derelict. The lighthouse since then has changed hands many times up to recent years, and it has been mainly used as a house. In 1954, the owners installed a spiral staircase in the tower so they could easily climb to the top and gaze out over the flat expanse of the Humber estuary. The property was on the market for £189,950 in February 2010, and reportedly sold for £145,000 the following year.

Grade II listed Paull lighthouse no longer stands on the shore, for a concrete defence wall now lies between the roadway alongside and the water. However, the carved stone plaque which reads "This lighthouse was built 1836 by the Trinity House of Kingston upon Hull – William Collinson; George Hall; Warden" can still be clearly read on its tower.

It has been said that the lighthouse is haunted by the ghost of a woman, with reports of footsteps in the tower, lights being turned on and off for no apparent reason, and objects moving of their own accord.

There have also been stories about tunnels leading from the lighthouse to the shore, the entrance having been blocked up long ago. Local people held that the tunnel had been used by smugglers.

The Humber Tavern in Paull briefly doubled up as a lighthouse.
TREV STANFORD

CHAPTER 32
SALT END

THE HAMLET OF Salt End on the north bank of the Humber in the parish of Preston on the eastern boundary of Hull, and a stone's throw from Paull, is dominated by the giant BP chemical works and a gas-fired power station. It also once had a pair of lighthouses.

As we have seen, the Brethren of Trinity House, Kingston upon Hull needed to replace Paull lighthouse due to changes in the course of the deepwater channel, and built two sets of lights, a pair at Thorngumbald Clough and another at Salt End.

In July 1870, the Salt End pair were built on the shore on land bought from the Humber Conservancy Commissioners, to a similar design to the Thorngumbald lighthouses on the opposite side of Paull.

Also built from wrought iron girders, the High Light comprised a 54ft red cylindrical tower standing on masonry foundations.

The lantern had a 50ft focal plane and, first powered by capillary wick oil lamps, was converted to electricity in 1926. A 300 candlepower single bulb shone its light through a holophote prismatic lens assisted by a prismatic reflector. The 150,000 candlepower beam of white light could be seen 12½ miles away. It displayed an occulting white light of four seconds and a two seconds eclipse, and a fixed white light as a guide to and from the three Killingholme lighthouses on the south shore of the Humber, and which are featured in my companion volume, *Lighthouses of the East Coast: East Anglia and Lincolnshire.*

The Low Light, a white 22ft wrought iron cylindrical tower with a 28ft focal plane, could, like its Thorngumbald Clough counterpart, also be moved 21ft along a railway track and laid in this case along a wooden jetty in front of the High Light.

It showed a fixed white light, with a subsidiary red sector light of five degrees divergence showing towards Skitter Sand Elbow light buoy. The light could be seen 10½ miles away.

The pair of lights were also controlled by a clockwork switch, to the same timings as the Thorngumbald Clough pair.

Both lights had become unattended by 1939, with no keeper employed to permanently look after them, and the keeper's cottage was rented out.

New jetties for the British Petroleum Oil Terminal were built in the 1960s. The Salt End lights became redundant at this time and were demolished, leaving no trace of them. Basic light poles on the three oil terminal jetties today fulfil a similar role.

The Salt End Low and High Lights and the keeper's cottage.
MIKE MILLICHAMP COLLECTION

CHAPTER 33
WHITGIFT

WHILE THE HUMBER estuary has by necessity many navigational marker lights and beacons, the only conventional tower lighthouse on the Ouse-Trent section is situated just north of the small linear village of Whitgift east of Goole.

This Grade II listed structure on the south bank of the Ouse was erected in the late 19th century for the Aire & Calder Navigation. Its octagonal unpainted stone base with ashlar cornice supports a white-painted circular tapered 46ft five-storey brick tower. The lantern has a balcony with timber decking and a sheet metal dome, and there is no keeper's cottage alongside.

The lighthouse has proved to be a vital landmark for ships going in and out of Goole Docks, Britain's most inland port, to and from the North Sea, warning them of the mudbanks at Whitgift Ness

Operated by the Port of Hull and Goole, it is very much active, showing a continuous red light, and has a focal plane of 39ft.

Run by Associated British Ports, Goole Docks has regular cargo liner services to Norway, Sweden, Finland, Germany, The Netherlands, Belgium, France, Spain, Morocco and South Africa. There is also trade by charter vessels to and from other countries, including Russia, Denmark and Italy, while cargo from other parts of the world such as United States of America, China and Australia reaches Goole by transshipment services from Rotterdam.

A dedicated rail freight terminal accommodates trainloads of cargo to and from the port, which handles around two million tons of cargo a year.

Whitgift once had an important ferry, remembered in the name of the former Angel and Ferry pub. The village church is famous for its clock, erected in 1919, which displays XIII instead of XII. It is said that either the painter had one pint too many in the pub or the original number was painted over at some stage, with the gilt of the original I showing through.

Whitgift marks the end of our journey which began on Berwick breakwater, and ends near the boundary of South Yorkshire and Lincolnshire.

My companion volume, *Lighthouses of the East Coast: East Anglia and Lincolnshire*, takes up the story from Apex Light, which once marked Trent Falls where that river joins the Ouse to become the Humber. The book then continues with the Killingholme lighthouses on the south bank of the Humber and follows the coast all the way into the inner Thames estuary.

There is a slight degree of overlap here. While Apex Light belongs historically to the next volume, it is now preserved at the Yorkshire Waterways Museum in Goole, which we have leapfrogged over in order to get to Whitgift.

The red-painted electricity-powered 40ft steel light on wooden pile foundations and with a 30ft focal plane and foghorn was built in 1933 by the Lower Ouse Improvement Trustees to improve navigation at the confluence of the two great rivers. Trent Falls takes its name from the rapid race of water at difficult states of the tide, which at certain times of the year, is funnelled up the Trent to create a tidal bore known as the Trent Aegir, similar to the Severn Bore.

Replaced by a basic navigational light mast on the old Blacktoft Jetty, Apex Light was moved to the museum which has been developed on the side of the Dutch River, where it now guards nothing busier than a model boat pond.

Lonely Whitgift lighthouse was built to improve
the safety of ships accessing Goole Docks.
ROBIN JONES

Whiftgift lighthouse on the south bank of the estuary of the River Ouse before it becomes part of the Humber. ROBIN JONES

Apex Light from Trent Falls at the Yorkshire Waterways Museum in Goole. ROBIN JONES